Nigel Scotland

Series Editor: Brian H Edwards

Day One

TRAVEL
THROUGH

Rome—City of empire, Christendom and culture

☉ In the steps of the apostle Paul

The massive cobbled stones of Via Appia Antica which leads in passed the catacombs of Sebastian, Calisto and Domitilla has a distinctly rural feel. This is the road on which Paul travelled to a martyr's death in the city

CONTENTS

© Day One Publications 2011 First printed 2011

A CIP record is held at The British Library   ISBN 978-1-84625-283-9

Published by Day One Publications Ryelands Road, Leominster, HR6 8NZ

🕿 01568 613 740 FAX 01568 611 473   email: sales@dayone.co.uk   www.dayone.co.uk   All rights reserved

Design: Kathryn Chedgzoy Printed by Polskabook, UK

Dedication: Liz my late dearly loved wife who loved this city

Welcome to Rome

A stay in Rome brings the visitor into close touch with the early Christian world. It was here shortly after the resurrection and ascension of Jesus that the early Christians began to establish a number of small congregations. It was here also that Peter and Paul, the two great apostles and leaders of the Christian church, lived for a time and died as martyrs in the persecution.

Rome wasn't built in a day, and it would be possible to spend months, indeed years, visiting and appreciating the many Christian sites, buildings, art and architecture. This travel guide is therefore inevitably selective, and the sites that it covers are particularly intended to give some detailed insights into early Christian worship and society. It will also make us aware of the intense persecution suffered by the early church in the years before the Emperor Constantine embraced the Christian faith in AD 312.

In the years following Constantine's conversion, Christianity became the established religion of the whole Roman Empire and enjoyed the patronage of the wealthy who built splendid, gracious buildings and became patrons of the arts and architecture. This travel guide will also take us to some of the most important of these places including St John Lateran, St Peter's Basilica, the Vatican Museums and the Villa Borghese and Park. This Renaissance cultural experience can be further enhanced by eating out in some of the gracious squares such the Piazza Navona, Piazza di Spagna with its famous Spanish steps and the Piazza di Trevi with its magnificent fountains. Welcome to the Eternal City.

Facing Page: A view over Rome

❶ Christianity comes to Rome

Rome was the capital of the empire in which the Christian faith originated. It was here that one of the earliest Christian churches was formed and here that the great apostles Peter and Paul both preached and presented the challenge of the Christian message to the pagan culture of the Roman world

It is not clear from the New Testament how Christianity first came to take root in Rome although there were Jews from Rome who were present in Jerusalem on the day of Pentecost (Acts 2:10). It seems that Paul's earliest link with the city was when he met with Priscilla and Aquila at Corinth. They had left the city when the Emperor Claudius expelled the Jews (Acts 18:2). Suetonius, the Roman historian, recorded that the trouble in Rome was caused by a certain 'Chrestus'. This is likely to be a variant of 'Christus', and in any event it is clear that Christianity had already reached Rome well before that time since, as we have seen, there were Jews from the city who were converted on the day of Pentecost.

A few years after he had become acquainted with Priscilla and Aquila, Paul decided he 'must also see Rome' (Acts 19:21). When he wrote his letter to the Romans shortly afterwards, his plan was to visit his friends in the city on the way to Spain (Romans 15:24). Paul had evidently known of

Christians in Rome for some time (Romans 15:23) and from his detailed greetings in chapter 16 he was clearly well acquainted with many of them. He knew that they were strong Christians whose faith was 'being reported all over the world' (Romans 1:8).

The Christians in Rome were a mixed community, a fact that is apparent from the greetings. Some were Jews, which is part

Above: Icon of the apostle Paul at St Peter's, Rome

Facing page: Statue of the apostle Paul at St John Lateran

Above: A view of the Appian Way

of the reason for the extended discussion about the future of Israel in chapters 9–11. Others who are listed in chapter 16 have Roman names such as Ampliatus (v 8), Urbanus (v 9), and Aristobulus (v 10). Andronicus and Junias (v 7) and Herodion (v 11) are apparently Paul's relatives. It is also of note that several women held positions of responsibility, notably Aquila a 'fellow-worker' (v 3), Mary 'who worked very hard for you'(v 6), Tryphena and Tryphosa 'women who work hard in the Lord' and Persis 'another woman who has worked very hard in the Lord'(v 12). Significantly, no one appears to be singled out as the sole leader of the church and Peter is nowhere mentioned, so clearly he was not in Rome at this time. When Paul himself finally arrived in Rome several years

later he was met on the way by the 'brethren' at the Forum of Appius (Acts 28:16). The last two verses in Acts recount that 'Paul stayed for two years in his own rented house and welcomed all who came to see him.' There he 'boldly and without hindrance preached the Kingdom of God and taught about the Lord Christ'

Peter in Rome?

The New Testament has no explicit reference to Peter's presence in Rome, although there are some possible hints that he went to the city at an early point in time. Romans 15:20–22 suggests that another apostle had been present in Rome before Paul went there. Peter may have been in Rome when he wrote: 'She who is in Babylon … sends you her greetings and so does my son Mark' (1Peter 5:13). This is likely a veiled reference to the fact that Peter is writing from Rome, 'Babylon' being a biblical symbol

Clement of Rome

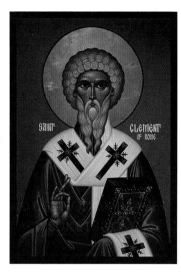

Right: Icon of Clement from the Church of St Paul-outside-the-Walls

Few details are known of Clement's life. He may well have been Paul's companion mentioned in Philippians 4:3. His Letter to the Corinthians, written shortly before his death in AD 96, is important because it is the first indication of the leader at Rome addressing with authority a Christian church in another part of the Roman Empire. The immediate reason for the letter was that the Corinthians had deposed some of their church leaders, and Clement called for their reinstatement. His letter shows that the same strife and divisions that Paul had encountered at Corinth were still in evidence. Clement writes of their 'envy and jealousy, strife and dissension, aggression and rioting, scuffles and kidnappings' and urges them 'to be done with these vapid fancies and return instead to the honourable, holy rule of our tradition.' In a later passage Clement says that 'there must be no time lost in putting an end to this state of affairs' and that 'those of you who were at the root of these disorders must make your submission to the clergy.'

Clement is venerated as a martyr although there is no certain evidence that he was. The story that he was sentenced to hard labour in Crimea and was lashed to an anchor and drowned in the sea is doubtful. If he was martyred, the likelihood is that he stood up for the truth of the Christian faith and died in consequence in the Colosseum. It was also claimed that he had great success in his missionary labours.

Left: The Temple of Vespasian was begun in the year he died (AD 79) as a means of honouring him as a son of the Roman deity

for Rome. Compare Revelation 17:5–6 which speaks damningly of 'Babylon the Great' being drunk with the blood of those who bore testimony to Jesus, and is generally agreed to be a reference to the martyrdoms in the imperial city. Certainly John Mark was a close companion of Paul when the apostle was a prisoner in Rome (Colossians 4:10), and he was also a co-worker with Peter, though whether in Rome or not is less certain.

Although there is no explicit reference in the New Testament to Peter having been present in Rome, in the late second century an historical tradition claims that Peter worked in Rome and died there as a martyr. The apocryphal *Acts of Peter*, though written too late to have come from the pen of Peter, relates that when the apostle was in Jerusalem, he was prompted by a vision to set out the next day for Caesarea where he would find a ship ready to sail for Italy. Peter responded immediately and was able to embark just as the ship was on the point of leaving. He then arrived at Rome via Puteoli where he ministered and was subsequently martyred uttering the words, 'I beseech you the executioners, crucify me thus, with the head downward and not otherwise.' The term 'pope' was not used until the time of Leo the Great, a fourth century Bishop of Rome, who referred to himself as 'Pappa' and began the idea of the supremacy of Peter.

The *First Letter of Clement* was written by Clement to the Christians in Corinth about AD 95. Clement was the leader of the church in Rome at the time, and he refers to Peter and Paul as 'heroes of more recent times' and 'pillars of our church'. He uses the Greek word 'martyrs' clearly implying that they were both put to death for their faith. About a hundred years later we have information that the earthly remains of Peter were buried on Vatican Hill and those of Paul on the road to Ostia. Recent Vatican excavations have revealed a tomb underneath the high altar in St Peter's Basilica which may be what Eusebius describes as the 'trophy' of Peter on Vatican Hill.

The tradition of the martyrdom of the apostles was given by Eusebius, the church historian, advisor to the emperor Constantine and Bishop of Caesarea. Writing in AD 327 in his *The Ecclesiastical History and the Martyrs of Palestine (History of the Church)*, he stated, 'It is recorded that in his [Nero's] reign Paul was beheaded in Rome itself, and that Peter likewise was crucified, and the record is confirmed by the fact that the cemeteries there are still called by the names of Peter and Paul.' Eusebius continued, 'I can point out the monuments of the victorious apostles. If you will go as far as the Vatican or the Ostian Way, you will find the monuments of those who founded this church.' Tradition gives the place of Paul's beheading as Tre Fontane and says that his body is buried where the Church of St Paul-outside-the-Walls now stands.

Right: The Colosseum in Rome where many Christians were martyred

Martyrs

Peter and Paul were two among many thousands of Christians who died for their faith in Jesus in the city of Rome. The majority were put to death in the Circus Maximus and in Nero's Circus. Some died in the Colosseum and elsewhere. Among the most noted martyrs were Ignatius, Justin and Callistus.

Ignatius (c 35–107) was the leader of the church at Antioch in Asia Minor. It was there, in what was a great centre of early Christianity, that he was sentenced to death by the Emperor Trajan and was sent to Rome to be thrown to the wild beasts at the public 'games'. He wrote a letter ahead of his arrival in the city in which he urged the Christians there not to try to get him reprieved: 'Leave me to imitate the passion of my God.' He is believed to have died in the Colosseum about 107 AD. Ignatius' death is recorded in *The Martyrdom of Ignatius* and is also reported by Eusebius in his *History of the Church*. See Box on Eusebius page 14.

Justin (100–165) was born at Shechem in Palestine from a Greek pagan family. He studied philosophy and became a Christian when he was in his early thirties. He remained a layman and travelled about preaching the gospel. Justin

Above: A cross in the Colosseum marks where the emperor sat

Top left: *Drawing of Justin Martyr by André Thévet (1516–1592), Chaplain to Catherine Medici*

Below left: *The catacomb of Callistus*

was an important apologist and wrote two *Apologies*, or defences of Christianity, to the persecuting Roman authorities setting out the moral values of the faith. Justin stayed in Rome twice and on the second occasion he was put to death by beheading, with five other men and women.

We now know that some of the persecuted Christians worshipped secretly in the catacombs and that a number of the early leaders of the Roman Church who were martyred were buried there. Among them were Fabian who was bishop from 236–250 and who was martyred during the persecution of the Emperor Decius, and Cecilia who since the sixteenth century has been regarded as the patroness of music. She founded a church in her home in the Trastevere quarter of the city. Around the year 230 AD Cecilia was martyred there beside her husband Valerian whom she had led to faith in Christ. Some five hundred years later her body was removed and placed in the new church which Pope Pascal had built over her supposed home.

Despite the harsh persecutions which it faced, the church in Rome continued to grow. Eusebius tells us that 'the blessed apostles [presumably Peter and or Paul] entrusted the episcopal office to Linus' who is mentioned by Paul in his Letter to Timothy (2 Timothy 4:21). Apart from the fact that Linus is alleged to

Above: The Ponte Fabricio is Rome's oldest working bridge. Built in 62BC it links the Jewish Quarter with Tiber Island

have been Bishop of Bésancon and stood against Menander, an opponent of Christianity, nothing else is known with certainty about him. Linus (67–76) was succeeded as Bishop of Rome by Anacletus (76–88) who is believed to have built a small chapel over the tomb of St Peter which was the structure over which the Emperor Constantine later erected the first great basilica in AD 324. After him, according to Eusebius, 'The blessed bishopric fell to Clement, who had seen the blessed apostles and conversed with them, and still had their preaching ringing in his ears and their authentic tradition before his eyes.' See Box on Clement of Rome page 9.

Left: The statue of St Cecilia by Stefano Maderno (1576–1636) in front of the main altar in the church of Santa Cecilia in Trastevere. Tradition claims that she was beheaded while making the sign of the Trinity. See also page 89

Eusebius (c 260–c349) 'The father of church history'

Eusebius became Bishop of Caesarea about the year AD 315 and is known as the 'father of church history'. His *History of the Church*, which he completed in AD 326, is the most significant of his many writing and carries the story of the Christian church from the time of the apostles to his own day. He became a close friend and adviser of the Emperor Constantine whose life he completed writing in AD 337. In both these books Eusebius recounted the vision of Jesus which Constantine had at the time of the battle of Milvian Bridge in AD 312 and his subsequent conversion and promotion of the Christian faith. Although some doubt has been shed on Eusebius' reliability, particularly because of his flattery of Constantine, there is no doubt that the emperor was a changed man and an active promoter of the Christian faith. Some of the details that Eusebius gives about Milvian Bridge have been corroborated by Lactantius and others. See Box on Constantine page 26.

The Christians in Rome grew rapidly in numbers in the second and third centuries. According to Eusebius, Justin 'tells us right up to his own time prophetic gifts were a conspicuous feature of the Church.' One of the more prominent and learned Christians in Rome was Hippolytus (died c 235). He was a bishop, but the precise location of his pastoral ministry is unknown. He seems not to have been too keen on the prophetic gifts and wrote several important

Below: Statue of St Peter outside St Peter's

books of which we still have copies. Among them was *Apostolic Tradition* in which he gives full details of the worship, disciplines and practices of Christians in early third century Rome. For example, he tells us that the Sunday Service was Holy Communion and included readings from the writings of the apostles, a sermon and prayers said over the bread and wine before they were given to the people. He also informs us that when baptism took place the candidates were exorcised and anointed with oil.

Later in the third century, the Bishop of Rome, Cornelius, wrote a letter to Bishop Fabius of Antioch in which he gave the following details of the church in his city: 'There are forty-six presbyters, seven deacons, seven sub-deacons, forty-two acolytes (helpers who assisted with the preparation of the bread and wine of Holy Communion), fifty-two exorcists, readers and doorkeepers, and more than fifteen hundred widows and distressed persons. All these are supported by the Master's grace and love for men.'

Lapsed Christians

One particular problem which many congregations in the city of Rome had to deal with during Cornelius' time was what to do about those who had denied Jesus during the times of persecution. Rather than face cruel death, many offered incense to the statues of emperors such as Nero and Domitian who proclaimed themselves to be divine. Some Christians obtained false certificates to say they had acknowledged the emperor as 'Lord', while others managed to persuade someone to make the necessary sacrifice on their behalf.

Cornelius followed in the footsteps of Jesus who forgave Peter after his threefold denial. Cornelius believed that after full public penitence the lapsed should be restored to fellowship. Others in the city supported another bishop, Novatian, who took a more rigorous line against those who had offered sacrifices to the emperor. Eventually sixty bishops and other clergy came together in the autumn of AD 251 and held a Synod which excommunicated Novatian.

The Christians in Rome continued to be persecuted well into the beginning of the fourth century. One of the harshest and most bitter periods of suffering and brutality began under Emperor Diocletian in February 303.

An edict was issued that Christians throughout the Empire had to recant or be punished. Churches were to be destroyed and sacred books and objects were to be confiscated. In this persecution many of the earliest manuscripts of the New Testament were destroyed. In AD 305 the brutal Diocletian fell ill and abdicated. His successor, Galerius, was Emperor from 305–311, and his rule also resulted in continued persecution for the Christian churches in various parts of the Empire.

Emperor Constantine

Galerius divided the Roman Empire into four areas, two in the East and two in the West, each with a provincial ruler. When he died, he left the Empire in the hands of all four provincial rulers and this resulted in a struggle for power. In AD 306 Constantine was serving with the legions in York, England when his father died and he was declared to be Emperor in the West. However Constantine's rival, Maxentius, moved his army into Rome and provisioned the city. Constantine responded with an immediate march on Rome with forty thousand troops gathered from Britain and France. Eusebius recorded that on reaching the outskirts of the city, Constantine 'invoked Jesus Christ in prayer as his aid' and 'saw with his own eyes a cross of light above the sun, and bearing the inscription, *in hoc signo vinces* [in this sign conquer]'. At this sight 'he himself was struck with amazement, and his whole army also, which followed him on this expedition, and witnessed this miracle.' Lactantius records that Constantine saw the chi-rho symbol; and this he painted on the shields of his legionaries. See Box: Early Christian symbols page 88 and Box: Constantine the Great page 26.

Maxentius, who had consulted the Sibylline Oracle, rashly came out of the city. He and many of his troops were drowned in the Tiber in the ensuing confrontation with Constantine's soldiers who rode into battle with the Christian emblem inscribed on their shields. It is claimed that Constantine never lost a battle with the chi-rho on his standard. Constantine then spent the winter in Milan where he met with Licinius, the main provincial

Below and inset: The statue of the Emperor Constantine at York, England

CONSTANTINE THE GREAT 274 – 337

Near this place, Constantine the Great was proclaimed Roman Emperor in 306. His recognition of the civil liberties of his Christian subjects, and his own conversion to the Faith, established the religious foundations of Western Christendom.

This statue was provided by the York Civic Trust and unveiled by the Rt Revd. and Rt Hon. Lord Coggan D.D., former Archbishop of York and of Canterbury on 25 July 1998.

Left: The Chi Rho symbol, being the first two letters of the Greek word for Christ. This is a coin of the emperor Magnentius c. AD 353 by which time it was common for the emperors to use the symbol

Below: Constantine at Milvian Bridge by Raphael. Vatican Museum

Inset: A coin of Constantine showing the chi-rho symbol above his standard (Labarum)

ruler in the East, and came to an understanding with him about dealing with the Christians. Their agreement, which was published in AD 313 and is known as *The Edict of Milan* granted full toleration to the Christians.

Following the battle of Milvian Bridge, Constantine championed the Christian faith in a manner that radically changed the history of the Roman Empire, if not world history. Constantine granted freedom of religion to all, but set Christianity on a privileged footing. All places of Christian worship which had been purchased or forcibly taken during the persecutions had to be returned without payment or any form of compensation. See Box on Constantine the Great page 26.

Among other things, Constantine issued more humane legislation to criminals and debtors, humanised the treatment of slaves and strengthened marriage, albeit with brutal treatment for unfaithfulness. He improved the status of the clergy who were exempted from tax collecting duties and were paid a salary by the state for their pastoral work and for organising public worship. In AD 320 Constantine introduced legislation which

suppressed soothsayers and divination. He financed new copies of the Bible, and in 321 declared Sunday to be a public holiday on which 'all factories and workshops' were closed, although farmers were allowed to work if the weather permitted! This meant that for the first time Sunday was a day when Christians were free from work and able to worship.

Constantine remained a strong and ruthless soldier, and a dictatorial emperor and politician. Nevertheless he had the Bible read in his residence every day and he wrote many letters with reference to Christ in them. Occasionally he gave sermons, and he took a keen interest in theological questions, most notably the debates about Jesus. He presided over the Council of Nicaea in AD 325 which declared that Jesus was God in all his fullness. His interference in church affairs was not always positive since he was often out of his depth when it came to theological matters!

Constantine brought his mother, Helena, to faith in Christ. Shortly after her conversion she visited the sites of Jesus' life and ministry in the Holy Land and in so doing became the inspirer of Christian pilgrimage there. Helena is widely believed to have brought a number of Christian artefacts back to Rome. These include supposed fragments of the true cross and the steps leading up to Pilate's Judgement Hall which Jesus ascended to his trial and suffering. These steps, known as the 'Scala Santa', are located in the Old Papal Palace beside St John Lateran.

When Helena returned from Israel she adapted several rooms in her palace as a chapel, and packed the floor with soil from Jerusalem which she brought as ballast in her ship. After her death the palace became Santa Croce (Holy Cross) Church. Despite the fact that it has a Baroque eighteenth century façade it is basically a Roman building which goes back before AD 325. This can be recognized easily by looking at the brickwork on the sides of the building. Since 1930 the relics have been transferred to a modern relic chapel where they can be seen. The entrance is near the end of the left aisle.

The supposed relics at Santa Croce include two thorns from the Crown of Thorns, a Roman nail and 'The Title of the Cross' which was alleged to have been found in the wall of the building in 1492 behind a brick inscribed with the words 'Titulis Crucis'. On the wood fragment the words 'Jesus of Nazareth, King' in Greek and Latin are still legible (see John 19:20). Another relic is the great beam said to be part of the penitent thief's cross. The story of the finding of Jesus' cross was not documented until the fourth century, some three hundred years after the event, when Bishop Cyril of Jerusalem referred in his catechism classes to particles of the true Cross being scattered throughout Christendom.

The place of relics

The practice of venerating relics was begun long after the time of the apostles, when prayer services were held over the tombs of the martyrs often on the anniversary of their deaths. In *The Martyrdom of Polycarp,* which was penned about the year AD156, the bones of Polycarp are described as 'more valuable than precious stones and finer than refined gold' and 'to be honoured by a memorial service for the saint at the place where they were laid.' From these beginnings there emerged a cult of relics in which it came to be believed that touching and venerating the remains of bodies that had been temples of the Holy Spirit conveyed healing, help and a variety of other benefits. At the time of the Crusades many relics, often spurious, were brought to Europe and placed in containers, known as reliquaries. The veneration of holy relics has remained a prominent feature in the life and worship of the Roman Catholic and Eastern Orthodox churches; however, many Christians believe that the plain teaching of the New Testament is that true worship is in spirit and truth (John 4:24) and that we are to pray, worship and have faith in Christ alone as our only intermediary with the Father. The biblical understanding is that when a person dies the body returns to the ground and 'the spirit to God who gave it' (Ecclesiastes 12:7) and that that there is no divine presence in anyone's mortal remains.

From Rome to Byzantium (Constantinople)

When Constantine moved east to take up residence in his new capital city of Constantinople, he gave the palace of his second wife, Fausta, to the bishops of Rome as a residence. It remained as such until it was badly damaged by fire in 1308. In his *History of the Church*, Eusebius wrote of 'the dedication festivals in the cities and consecrations of the newly built places of worship.' Among the many churches which were constructed in Rome following Constantine's Edict of Toleration were St John, Lateran, San Clemente, St Peter in the Vatican and St Paul-outside-the-Walls. Constantine personally instructed the building of the first St Peter's much of which, up to about half of the walls in height, is still in existence. The reason for this is that the new building was constructed on the old foundations. It is almost certain that the emperor also ordered the construction of a small church over Paul's tomb in a cemetery beside the road to Ostia. There is testimony to this fact in the writings of Josephus and others. About fifty years afterwards, Emperor Valentinian replaced it with an impressive basilica which is basically the one we see today although it was restored after a major fire in July 1823. The cloisters survived the fire intact.

After Constantine had left Rome to establish a new capital for the empire at Byzantium, the church managed to take advantage of the prestige still attached to the city. It absorbed some of the imperial practices and terminology. 'Diocese' was an administrative area in a Roman province, and 'parish' comes from the Greek word *paroikia* and literally meant the immediate area surrounding the house of the local magistrate.

Above: *Artist's impression of the first St Peter's as it was in medieval times*

Above: *Mass at St Peter's Square*

Christians took over some of the state functions such as the relief of the poor, caring not simply for Roman citizens but also for all the needy of the city.

In the fifth century, with the military might of the empire fading, the church remained and became steadily more influential as its monks evangelized the territories of Europe. What once had been the Roman Empire, dominated by the emperors, became instead the 'Holy Roman Empire' ruled over by the bishops of Rome. Some of their number, such as Innocent I (401–417) and Leo the Great (440–461),

became very powerful. Leo proved to be a competent biblical theologian who helped the Christian churches as a whole to understand that Jesus is both fully human and fully God. This enabled the great Council which met at Chalcedon in AD 451 to declare that Jesus is fully at one with God the Father in every way, and at the same time fully human, at one with our humanity in every way. This was not a new or novel theology, but a clear statement of what the majority of churches across the empire had always believed.

TRAVEL INFORMATION

All the sites and buildings mentioned in this first introductory chapter are considered in detail in the succeeding chapters where travel information and advice is given together with opening times and street maps.

❷ Ancient empire and modern Italy

The Romans and their empire have had a major and lasting impact on the culture and the Christian faith of Europe. Nowhere is the power and magnificence of that influence more readily reflected than in the city of Rome. Still to this day the remains of the Forum reflects something of that former splendour and greatness

The details concerning the earliest history of ancient Rome are unknown for certain. They are further obscured by the legend of the city's foundation by Romulus allegedly in 753 BC. What we do know, however, is that the Republic came into being in 510/509 BC and took its authority from a Senate that was ruled by two consuls. In the same century Rome began to conquer some of the neighbouring territories until eventually the entire Italian peninsular became one federated whole. In the two Punic Wars of 246–241 BC and 218–202 BC further incursions were made into Sicily and parts of Spain and elsewhere. Finally, Macedonia and the Syrian kingdoms were taken, Carthage was destroyed and Greece was conquered, thus making Rome ruler of the entire Mediterranean lands.

These victories were followed by a series of internal conflicts in one of which Julius Caesar was murdered and, after the sea Battle of Actium in 31 BC in which Octavian defeated Antony and Cleopatra and became the undisputed ruler of Rome,

Octavian took the title Augustus. This title meant 'revered' and implied veneration as a son of the gods. The long reign of Augustus lasted from 27 BC to AD 14 and enabled him to organise the empire with a huge network of roads, forts and public buildings. In this period poetry, philosophy,

Above: *A model reconstruction of Ancient Rome with the Circus Maximus in the foreground, by Rudolfo Lanciani (1893–1901)*

Facing page: *The Rome Forum showing the glories of the ancient Roman Empire*

rhetoric and history flourished in the writings of men such as Horace, Virgil, Catullus, Ovid, Cicero, Livy and Tacitus. At the same time the Roman Empire absorbed all that was considered best in Greek art and culture, including the Greek deities which were given Latin names. For example the goddess Artemis, so loved and worshipped in Ephesus, became Diana.

The coming of Christianity

Jesus Christ was born in the reign of Augustus, and the apostles of Christ later spread his teachings throughout the Empire, a task which was made all the easier on account of the Roman peace, the universal Greek language and the growing network of roads. Christianity reached Rome at an early point as we saw in chapter one, and the apostles Peter and Paul were martyred in the city during the reign of the Emperor Nero. The Empire continued to expand until the reign of Trajan (AD 98–116). In the early years when the number of Christians was relatively small, persecution was sporadic and mostly at the hands of insecure emperors such as Domitian and Nero. Later however, as the number of Christians increased, the Roman persecutions became widespread and much more intensive and particularly so in Rome itself, the capital city.

The situation for the Christian church finally changed when, with the Edict of Milan in AD 313, Constantine allowed Christians the freedom to practise their faith openly and to erect official church buildings. Constantine later moved the capital of the empire from Rome to the ancient Greek city of Byzantium which he rebuilt and renamed Constantinople, meaning 'Constantine's City'—*polis* being the Greek word for city. The new capital was situated on the Bosphorus in modern Turkey (known today as Istanbul) and this eventually resulted in the empire dividing into east and west often with two emperors vying for power. For a while the western capital was moved to Milan which it was felt would offer better defences. However the

Right: Romulus Augustulus, the last western Roman emperor

Above: Romulus and Remus suckled by a she wolf

western empire was by now much more vulnerable and Rome was repeatedly sacked by Goths and Vandals and was finally overrun when Romulus Augustulus was defeated by Odacer in AD 476. From this time forward the bishops became the real rulers of Rome, and much of the western church and empire remained under Rome's papal dominance until the nineteenth century. However, the eastern empire continued to function until the final sack of Constantinople by the Islamic armies in May 1453.

Rome and western Christianity after the Empire

Christianity remained the official religion of the west, and under the influence of strong popes, such as Leo I (c 390–461), a number of the invading Gothic rulers embraced the Christian faith and culture. At the same time Christianity began to spread rapidly across Europe as a result of the growth of the monasteries. In this movement St Benedict (c 480–457), who founded the great monastery of Monte Cassino in Italy, was a significantly influential figure. From the latter half of the sixth century to the late seventh century Italy was ruled by the kings of the northern province of Lombardy who converted to Christianity. However, the popes came to resent their authority and called on the Franks to fight them. Thus Charlemagne (742–814) defeated the Lombard ruler Desiderius in 774. Italy now came under Carolingian (successors of Charlemagne) rule. Carolingian influence reached its peak on Christmas Day 800 when Pope Leo III crowned Charlemagne King of Italy and Holy Roman Emperor. This began an institution which was to last almost a thousand years, though critics often conclude that strictly speaking it was neither holy, Roman nor an empire.

Constantine the Great

Constantine (274–337) became Roman Emperor in AD 312 and was the son of Helena and Constantius Chlorus, a Roman Army officer and later Governor of Dalmatia. Educated in the court of the Emperor Diocletian, he imbibed the ideas of absolute rule. In 305 he joined his father's British campaign at York. On his father's death, Constantine was granted the title 'Caesar' with responsibility for Britain, Gaul and Spain. When Emperor Galerius died, Constantine's position was challenged by Maxentius who retreated into Rome and provisioned the city with African grain. A celebrated battle took place in 312 outside the city at Milvian Bridge at which Constantine's smaller forces routed Maxentius' army, many of whom, including Maxentius himself, were drowned in the Tiber. (See also page 16). Constantine entered Rome amidst

Above: *Emperor Constantine in the Capitoline Museum*

popular jubilation. Constantine fully supported the Christian church and granted privileges to the clergy. He established himself and his successors as the dominant authority over the church. He divided the Empire into two when he founded a new capital at Byzantium which he renamed Constantinople. The Eastern Empire proved much more lasting, surviving to the fifteenth century. During his lifetime, and that of his sons, Constantine was extolled as the ideal powerful but Christian ruler, though later accounts were less enthusiastic and portrayed him as a politician who manipulated and bullied all parties to secure his own position. This is an ongoing debate. There is no doubt that he was an active worshipping Christian, but on the other hand he was a powerful and at times ruthless military commander and emperor.

In the 13th and 14th centuries Italy became increasingly fragmented as cities such as Florence, Milan and Naples grew in wealth and power and began to challenge the authority of the church over their territories. Despite the political turmoil and struggles, the Italian states became great centres of Renaissance art and culture; this was seen in the work of men such as Michelangelo, Bernini, Borromini, Caravaggio and Tiepolo. In Rome many of the popes and cardinals of the Counter Reformation—the movement that began in 1545 to counter Luther and Protestantism—were great patrons of art, sculpture and painting. Many Baroque churches were built in the city during this time; the precise meaning of the word Baroque is still an open debate but it refers to the art and architecture of the 16th to 18th centuries. During the seventeenth and eighteenth centuries various European powers, including Spain and Austria, overran individual Italian territories, particularly those in the north.

The birth of modern Italy

The revolutionary upheavals in Europe in 1848 and the Crimean War from 1853–56 presented the Italian states with the opportunity to make an alliance with France and break free from Austrian control. Led by General Giuseppe Garibaldi, patriots such as the politicians Giuseppe Mazzini, Camillo Cavour, and the writer Alessandro Manzoni, struggled and eventually succeeded in creating a unified Italy. The new kingdom was proclaimed under King Victor Emmanuel II of Savoy in 1861 with its capital in Turin. Further fighting took place in 1866 which resulted in the annexation of Venice and the liberation of Rome from papal control in 1870.

Pope Pius IX, who had been in office since 1846, was 'imprisoned' within the walls of the Vatican. Pius formally pronounced the doctrine of the Immaculate Conception of the Virgin Mary in 1854 and Papal Infallibility in 1870—they had long been doctrines within the church but Pius now enforced them as canon law. Pius never accepted the incorporation of the papal states and Rome into the kingdom of Italy. The 'Roman Question' dragged on and was not finally settled until 1929 when the 'Lateran Pacts' were signed between the Holy See led by Pope Pius XI and the Italian government led by the fascist dictator Benito Mussolini. The Italian government agreed to recognize the sovereignty of the Vatican City State and

Below: Bernini's colonnaded Vatican Square

Left: Lithograph of Garibaldi fighting in the Battle of Rome

Below: Portrait of Garibaldi in 1861

the smallest nation in the world. It is situated at the heart of Rome on Vatican Hill with a recorded population of 921 in 2009. Its territory is less than a square mile. It is the headquarters of the Roman Catholic Church and its major buildings are St Peter's Basilica, the Vatican Museums, the Sistine Chapel and the Castel Sant Angelo, the papal fort.

Roman deities

When the Romans took over the Greek empire in the first century BC they adopted many of the Greek gods and gave them Roman names. The deities were represented in human form and temples were built in honour of many in the Forum and in other places in major towns and cities. Priests would pray to these statues seeking, for example, divine favour in battle, the subsidence of the flooding Tiber river or an improved harvest. Men and women visited the temple whose deity corresponded to their own particular need of the moment, and sacrifices were made to persuade the gods to grant particular requests. They also offered sacrifices of thanksgiving which included cattle, sheep and pigs. Animals were killed by

made financial compensation to the church for the loss of its territories. The Curia (papal government) still owns a number of churches outside the Vatican, including Santa Maria Maggiore, San Giovanni in Laterano and San Paolo fuori le Mura, together with the Pope's summer residence on Lake Albano.

The invasion of 1870 brought to an end the temporal power of the papacy except for their control over Vatican City which is now

Vatican City

The Vatican employs approximately 2,000 people and is a city state within the city of Rome. It was eventually established in 1929 after the papal lands had been taken over by the newly formed kingdom of Italy. While legislative authority rests with a group of cardinals who are appointed for a five year term, the Pope has absolute and full legislative and judicial authority over the territory. There are departments which are responsible for health, security and telecommunication. The Vatican has its own bank and issues its own coins. Since 1506 Swiss soldiers have formed a papal guard while the military defence of Vatican City is provided by the Italian armed forces. The Vatican city state is separate from the Curia which is the name given to the governing body that administer the worldwide Roman Catholic Church.

cutting the throat and allowing the blood to drain over the altar. Sacrificial meat was then shared by the priests and their assistants. Initiated followers of particular religions probably honoured their deities on special occasions with feasting and rituals. Many Romans also believed in household spirits, and families would make food and drink offerings to the household gods. On occasions a place was set for the god or goddess at the family table and a portion of food set aside for his or her use.

Chief among the Roman gods was Jupiter and a famous temple was erected in his honour on the Capitoline Hill in the centre of Rome. Following his victory over the men of Caenina about the year 750 BC, Romulus vowed to build a temple in honour of Jupiter, but it was never built in his lifetime. In 510 BC Lucius Superbus finally constructed the first building. The last structure was erected in the reign of Emperor Domitian (AD 81–96) which stood until it began to fall into ruins in the fifth century AD. Throughout the pre-Christian era, whenever a victorious Roman army returned to the city there was a triumphal procession to this temple of Jupiter, at the end of which the general, dressed to resemble Jupiter, offered a sacrifice in his honour. All that remains of Domitian's building can be seen behind the Palazzo dei Conservatori in an exhibition area built in the Caffarelli Garden. However, it was not only in Rome that Jupiter was honoured. As the supreme defender of the empire, he was also worshipped on hills and other places where nothing intervened between earth and heaven.

In addition to the adopted Greek gods, some Roman emperors themselves took divine status as a son of the gods and had temples built in their own personal honour. This became a major challenge to Christians when everyone was required to offer incense and declare that the emperor was Lord. Many hundreds of Christians preferred to suffer and even die rather than dishonour Jesus whom they believed to be the one and only Lord.

Above: Diana as the huntress in the Vatican

The more important Roman deities

This section gives a brief introduction to the most important Roman deities and their particular roles and functions. Although most of the temples that were erected in their honour were gradually destroyed with the 'Christianizing' of the empire, there are some significant remains in various parts of the city. As these are scattered in several different areas, it is probably best to explore them while you are visiting the various Christian sites which are covered in the following chapters. They are marked on the travel sections

Apollo was the son of Zeus and Leto and twin brother of Diana (Artemis). Zeus was the god of the Sun and Sunday was his special day. Apollo was held to be the god of social and intellectual attributes and also of healing. The main centre of Apollo was at Delphi, but there was a temple of Apollo in Rome. It stands just a few feet away from the walls of the Theatre of Marcellus, on the edge of the Jewish quarter. All that remains are three Corinthian columns on which rests a corner section of architrave. The remains of another temple of Apollo can be found on the Palatine. Overlooking the Circus Maximus, it adjoins the house of Augustus who dedicated it.

Diana (Artemis in Greek mythology), was the Roman goddess of the Moon, hence Monday was her special day. She is depicted carrying a bow and arrows as she was also the goddess of hunting. She is said to be the goddess of chastity, childbirth and little children. The centre of her cult was in Ephesus, a fact born out in Acts 19:27. There was a temple in honour of Diana on the Aventine Hill but nothing remains of it. In 1789 a replica of the ancient temple was constructed in the Borghese Park which is worth a stop on the way to the Gallery Borghese.

Aesculapius, the son of Apollo and Coronis, was the god of medicine and healing and in 293 BC a temple was built in his honour on Tiber Island when a severe plague hit the city. In 998 the Emperor Otto built the Church of Bartholomew over the ruins of the temple.

Bacchus (Dionysius in Greek mythology), the god of wine and fertility and the son of Zeus and Semele.

Castor and Pollux (Dioscuri and Polydeuces in Greek mythology), were Greek gods, the twin sons of Leda by Zeus. They were believed to be the protectors of mariners. See Acts chapter 28:11. The first temple in their honour in Rome was built in the Forum and dedicated about the year 484 BC. It has been rebuilt several times. The three surviving columns date from the Emperor Tiberius' reconstruction in 12BC

Above: Remains of the Temple of Castor and Pollux in the Forum

Below: Statue of Juno in the Capitoline Museum

Ceres (Demeter in Greek mythology), was the Roman goddess of tillage and corn. Her temple on the Avatine Hill was a popular cult centre with the labourers.

Cupid (Eros in Greek mythology), was the Roman god of love and was represented by an irresponsible cherub with a bow and arrow. Anyone hit by one of his arrows fell madly in love.

Fortuna (Tyche in Greek mythology), was originally associated with fertility and was the Roman goddess of wealth. She is represented with a cornucopia (horn-shaped container) and a ship's rudder.

Hercules (Heracles in Greek mythology), the son of Zeus and Alceme, was the god of strength and courage. His temple is located close to the Tiber in the Forum of Boarius close to the Ponte Palatino.

Isis, the wife of Osiris, the Egyptian goddess of the sky and

protector of the dead, was also popular in the Graeco-Roman world as the ideal mother.

Juno (Hera in Greek mythology), was the principal goddess in Roman mythology. The wife of Jupiter, she was concerned with all aspects of women's lives including their sexuality. The remains of a temple of Juno have been found in the ruins of the church of San Nicola Carcere on the edge of the Jewish quarter in Rome.

Jupiter (Zeus in Greek mythology), was the chief god of the Romans. Hence the Temple of Jupiter dominated the Forum in Rome and temples in his honour were prominently situated in many other towns and cities. The son of Saturn, he was the god of the sky associated with lightning and thunderbolts. Jupiter was believed to be the protector in battle and the bestower of victory. He married his sister Juno. After Barnabas had healed a crippled man in the town of Lystra (Acts 14:11) the inhabitants of the town were so impressed that they called him Zeus. Most of the remains of the original temple are buried under the Nuovo wing of the Capitoline Museum.

Mars (Aries in Greek mythology), the father of Romulus and the greatest god after Jupiter, is the god of war and is represented as a fully-armed warrior. He is honoured in several festivals in March which is named after him. In Acts 17:22 Luke records that Paul debated just outside the city of Athens on Mars Hill which in the Greek is literally *Aries pagos* (Areopagus in the

Above: The statue of Eros in the Capitoline Museum

Below: Bust of the Emperor Tiberius in the Vatican

NIV translation and Mars Hill in the King James Version). The remains of the Temple of Mars are located in the Forum of Augustus.

Mercury (Hermes in Greek mythology), the son of Jupiter (Zeus) and Maia, is represented with a staff, winged shoes and a broad hat. He is the patron of merchants, travellers and roads and was believed to guide the

Below: The bust of Jupiter in the Capitoline Museum. Jupiter was chief among the Roman gods

deceased to the underworld. The people of Lystra gave Paul the name Hermes when, together with Barnabas, he had healed a crippled man. See Acts 14:11. The Temple of Mercury was situated between the Avantine and Palatine hills close to the Circus Maximus.

Minerva (Athena in Greek mythology), was the Roman goddess of intelligence, wisdom and of the handcraft arts. From the earliest days of Ancient Rome there was a temple to her on the Capitoline Hill near the temple of Jupiter.

Mithras, the Persian god of light who represented the power of goodness and promised his followers compensation for the present evil after death. Mithras was said to have captured and killed the sacred bull from whose blood all life sprang. Mithras was introduced into Roman society in 68 BC and by about AD 250

Mithras rivalled Christianity in parts of the empire. Mithras was the god of the Roman military and was honoured and worshipped by the Roman legions. There is a shrine to Mithras in the excavated area beneath the church of San Clemente.

Neptune (Poseidon in Greek mythology), was the god of the sea and also earthquakes. He carries a trident which has three prongs of the kind used by fishermen in the ancient world indicating his mastery of the seas.

Pluto (Orcus in Greek mythology), the brother of Zeus, was believed to be the god of the underworld. He was also worshipped as the god of the dead.

Saturn (Cronus in Greek mythology), was the god of agriculture and harvests. He was dethroned by his sons Jupiter, Neptune and Pluto. At his festival, the Saturnalia in December, gifts were exchanged and slaves were briefly treated as their master's equal. This festival was the prototype of the modern Christmas! The remains of his temple are in the Forum.

Venus (Aphrodite in Greek mythology), the mother of Aeneas, was born in the sea and first came ashore at Cyprus floating on a scallop

Above: The bust of Mithras the bull god from St Stephen Walbrook in London

Above: The Temple of Venus in the Forum

Below: Image of Christian Emperor Theodosius from the Missorium of Theodosius. Probably made in AD 388, now preserved in Real Academia de Historia, Madrid

shell. Originally the goddess of gardens, she later became the goddess of love. The impressive remains of her temple in Rome dominate the Forum.

Vesta, the goddess of light and the hearth, was worshipped in every Roman house. In the Temple of Vesta in Rome a sacred fire was kept burning day and night by six vestal virgins (meaning dedicated to Vesta) who were daughters of noble families. Vestals had to live in the House of the Vestal Virgins, and they served the temple for thirty years after which they returned to private life. The penalty for breaking their vow of chastity was burial alive. The remains of her temple occupy a central position in the Forum.

The worship of these Roman deities was finally brought to an end in AD 392 when the Christian Roman emperor, Theodosius I, banned the practice of pagan religions altogether.

TRAVEL INFORMATION

The temples of the Roman deities can be visited as you go to the various sites which are detailed in the following sections. If you wish to take a full day, the majority of them can be seen by visiting the Forum and the area in the vicinity of Tiber Island. There are also some temple remains in Largo Argentina. The deities have not as yet been precisely identified. The following maps will prove helpful.

Left: The Temple of Apollo

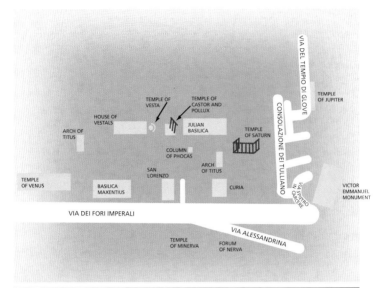

MAP OF THE TEMPLES IN THE FORUM AREA

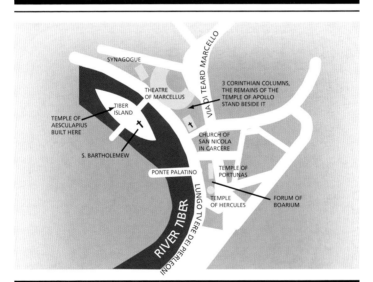

MAP OF THE TEMPLES IN THE TIBER ISLAND AREA

The Forum is easily reached by taking the Metro line B to Colosseo and there are numerous buses which pass along the Via del Fori Imperiali.

The Tiber area is also easily reached by bus from Termini and elsewhere. The Tiber area can also be reached by taking the Metro line B to Circo

Massimo and by walking along the Via del Circo Massimo and turning right and walking a few hundred meters along the river bank.

❸ In the steps of the martyrs

'I am God's wheat, ground fine by lions' teeth to be made purest bread for Christ'. So wrote Ignatius, the pastor of the church at Antioch as he journeyed to his death in Rome

To visit the Colosseum, the Circus Maximus, the Jewish quarter and the Pantheon is to walk in the steps of the early Christian martyrs who suffered brutality and death at the hands of the persecuting Roman authorities. Constantine's arch, erected following his conversion to the Christian faith, marks the end of this cruel chapter.

The Colosseum

The Colosseum, or Flavian Amphitheatre to give it its correct name, is one of the world's most famous monuments. The building was begun in AD 70 by the Emperor Vespasian who used many of the thousands of Jews captured at the fall of Jerusalem as forced labour. This fact is depicted by the sculptured motifs on the inside of the Arch of Titus in the Forum. Initially, it was thought that the name 'Colosseum' arose from the building's vast size but many historians believe that its designation referred to a 'colossal' statue of the Emperor Nero (the Colossus) which stood nearby. The base of the pedestal on which this Colossus stood is still visible just across the road from the Metro Station.

The eighth century English historian, the Venerable Bede, is believed to be the first to have written of this vast edifice as the 'Colisaeus'. Vespasian, who had been a professional soldier, held a particular dislike for his megalomaniac and deranged predecessor, Nero. He therefore destroyed Nero's statue, drained Nero's artificial lake and erected the Colosseum in its place.

The purpose of the building was to satisfy the appetite of the Roman populace for games and sports, and to please the gods who were believed to be watching from Olympus; this

Above: *Showing the remains of the base of the Colossus of Nero*

Facing page: *The Colosseum, a centre for tourism*

was the origin of the Olympic games from the eighth century BC. Everything which the Romans built had to be bigger and better than anything else, and this accounts for the expansive nature of the Colosseum. It is a huge elliptical construction over 45.7m (150ft) high. It is built of good quality limestone and the foundations reach twelve metres below ground. The central enclosed arena is 87.4m long (287ft) by 54.8m wide (180ft). During the 1999–2000 restoration, archaeologists found evidence that the arena was covered with 3,588 square yards of wooden flooring. The Colosseum was entered through 80 separate arched entrances, 76 of which were for the ordinary people, two for the emperor and two for the gladiators. It could seat 55,000 spectators on five different levels. The emperor sat on a podium within a marble terrace, together with the Vestal Virgins. The second floor was for women and the middle classes. Above the top level there was a huge awning which was supported on 240 wooden poles. This would be

Above: *The bust of Nero*

Below: *The remains of the gladiatorial school beside the Colosseum*

drawn across with ropes by sailors in order to keep the sun off the audience. A hundred sailors, who were used to climbing high masts and dealing with ropes, were always in attendance especially for this task. Below the floor level

there were a whole host of chambers in which prisoners and wild animals, including bears and big cats, were kept. The wild beasts were winched up to the arena by a series of pulleys.

The first audiences visited the Colosseum in AD 80, and the opening was marked by a hundred days and nights of celebration, games and festivities. The games usually followed a set structure which began with a parade of chariots and a number of bloodless duels. This was followed by gladiators who were escorted into the arena. Those who lost their fights, if still alive, had to appeal to their opponents for mercy and they either spared or condemned them. If the emperor was present, the defeated gladiator could appeal to him for mercy. He often took advice from the crowd. If the crowd held their 'thumbs down' it meant death. If they gave the 'thumbs up' it meant freedom. In addition to the gladiatorial combats there were many fights between convicted prisoners and wild beasts. Statistics of just one celebration alone held in AD 248 record the slaughter of 30 elephants, 10 elk, 10 tigers, 70 lions, 30 leopards, 10 hyenas, 19 giraffes, 20 wild asses, 40 wild horses, 1 hippopotamus, 1 rhinoceros and two thousand gladiators! The organizers of the games constantly searched the length and breadth of the empire to supply new men and animals for these occasions.

Above: Exterior of the Colosseum as it is today

During the late first century and as late as the early fourth century, many Christians suffered death in the Colosseum. However, the great majority of Christians died in the Circus Maximus and in Nero's Circus. One of the most famous early Christian martyrs to die in the arena was Ignatius. According to Origen and Eusebius he was the leader of the church at Antioch in Asia Minor. Ignatius was personally interrogated by the Emperor Trajan who condemned him to walk to his death in Rome. This meant a journey of about three thousand miles during which he was accompanied by a detachment of ten Roman soldiers. Tradition claims that at the end he was thrown to wild beasts in the Colosseum. The year was probably AD 107. During his ordeal he was roughly treated by the soldiers 'who grow more insolent the more gratuities they are given'. Ignatius compared them to leopards.

As his journey progressed through Asia Minor many

Ignatius (c35–c107)

Little is known of the life of Ignatius (even his dates are uncertain) apart from the fact that he was the leader of the church at Antioch and one of the early Christian martyrs. He was held in high esteem by many early Christian leaders on account of the letters he wrote on his way to martyrdom. While he was in Smyrna he wrote to the churches at Rome, Ephesus, Magnesia and Tralles. He was then taken on to Troas where he wrote three further letters: two to the churches of Philadelphia and Smyrna and one to the Christian leader Polycarp. The following extract demonstrates his passionate devotion to Christ.

'For my part, I am writing to all the churches and assuring them that I am truly in earnest about dying for God—if only you yourselves put no obstacles in the way. I must implore you to do me no such kindness; pray leave me to be a meal for the beasts, for it is they who can provide my way to God. I am wheat, ground fine by the lion's teeth to be made purest bread for Christ. Better still, incite the creatures to become a sepulchre for me; let them not leave the smallest scrap of my flesh, so that I need not be a burden to anyone after I fall asleep. When there is no trace of my body left for the world to see, then I shall truly be Jesus Christ's disciple. ...

How I look forward to the lions that have been got ready for me! All I pray is that I may find them swift. ...This is the first stage of my discipleship; and no power, visible or invisible, must grudge me my coming to Jesus Christ (Ignatius **The Epistle to the Romans** section 4–5).

Above: *The martyrdom of Ignatius*

representatives from churches on his route came out to encourage him. For his part, Ignatius spent his evenings writing letters of encouragement to many of these local churches. He wrote wonderful things such as: 'He who is near to the sword is near to God'.

Christians found the martyrdoms and blood sports which took place in the Colosseum very disturbing and for the most part they stayed away. In AD 404 an eastern monk named Telemachus threw himself into the arena in an attempt to try and halt the bloodshed—and was stoned to death. The death of St Telemachus is commemorated on 1st January each year.

After Constantine's conversion, the gladiatorial games were increasingly opposed and they were finally brought to an end in AD 438. The last

Above: *The interior of the Colosseum showing the seating and underground area where the animals were kept*

Left: *Telemachus seeking to end gladiatorial combat in the Colosseum from* Foxe's Book of Martyrs

recorded animal slaying took place in AD 523. After this time the Colosseum fell into disrepair and the popes began to use the stone for their many building projects. Large numbers of marble statues were also burned in the 15th and 16th centuries to make lime which was the main binding agent for the brick and stone construction work. In addition to this, during the Middle Ages a series of earthquakes caused the Colosseum to fall into further ruin. An eighteenth century picture by the artist Canaletto shows the building in a seriously depleted condition. Many palaces and other public buildings were erected using its stone. In 1749 Pope Benedict XIV consecrated the Colosseum to the memory of the martyrs who died there and installed the stations of the cross in the building. Today, beside the imperial box, there is a plain wooden Cross. On the evening of Good Friday, Italians flock to the Colosseum to follow 'the way of the cross'. In 1807 restoration work began and has continued ever since.

Above: The Christians' last prayer by Jean-Léon Gérom in the Walters Art Gallery, Baltimore, USA

The Arch of Constantine

Constantine's Arch, which stands on the road running from the Colosseum to the Circus Maximus, is the largest triumphal arch in the city of Rome. It was constructed to celebrate

Above: Painting of the Colosseum by Giovanni Canaletto in the Borghese Gallery

Constantine's famous victory over Maxentius at the battle of Milvian Bridge which took place on 28 October 312. See page 16. The Arch was erected by order of the Senate and dedicated to the emperor on 25 July 315. The inscription on the top middle panel reads: 'To Emperor Caesar Flavius Constantius Maximus Pius Felix Augustus, the Senate and the People of Rome dedicated an arch decorated with triumphal representations because through divine inspiration and great wisdom, with his army and just arms he freed the state from the tyrant [Maxentius] and all factions'. Many scholars have interpreted the words 'divine inspiration' (*instinctu divinitas*) as a reference to Constantine's conversion.

The whole monument with its three arches was decorated with marble slabs. Many were plundered from other monuments in the imperial city. On the main faces and the ends of the shorter arches, at the level immediately above the apex of the arches, there are scenes from Constantine's campaign. On the west side we have Constantine departing with his army from Milvian Bridge. On the south side there is the siege of Verona, followed by the battle of Milvian Bridge. On the east side we have Constantine's triumphal entry into Rome. On the north side there is a representation of his speech to the crowd from the rostra in the Forum. The rest of the images on the arch, taken from other sources, are from the ages of Trajan, Hadrian and Marcus Aurelius and are devoid of Christian content.

The Circus Maximus

This is the largest and oldest circus in Rome. It is set between the Palatine and Aventine hills. Tradition says that it was founded by Tarquinius Priscus, the first Etruscan king of Rome, around 600 BC. In biblical terms this would be around the time of the Old Testament prophet Jeremiah, shortly after the death of King Josiah. That said, the earliest mention of the circus is in 329 BC which would be in the inter-Testamental period. From that point onwards we know that it has been enlarged and rebuilt many times. At its peak it could hold 380,000 spectators. The last games in the circus were held by the Ostrogoth King Totila in AD 549.

During the first four centuries following the birth of Christ, the Circus played host to a variety of entertainments that included athletic contests, wild beast fights and even mock naval battles for which purpose the circus was

Below: Constantine's triumphal arch

Bottom: Detail of the panel showing Constantine's troops outside Rome

flooded. The major function for which the Circus was designed was chariot and horse racing. The contest was usually seven circuits round the *spina*, a long low platform that ran down the centre of the circus. At either end of the spina there was a conical pillar known as a *meta*. These points were often the scene of serious accidents as charioteers turned sharply in an effort to gain ground on their opponents. The charioteers were organised into four teams, red, white, blue and

Left: Mosaic of chariot racing. Displayed in the Colosseum

Below: A Mosaic of gladiators

Bottom: The site of the Circus Maximus and spina as it is today

green and there was intense rivalry between them. The races often provoked extreme emotions, and fights sometimes broke out among the spectators who behaved in the manner of football rowdies on the terraces; there was also much betting by the Roman populace on the outcome of the chariot races.

The significance of the Circus for early Christianity is that this was the place where more Christians suffered and died for their faith than anywhere else in Rome. Probably the full extent of the suffering and death that took place here will never be known. Writing of the martyrdoms, the Roman historian Tacitus spoke of there being 'vast numbers in Rome'. Clearly we are talking of many thousands. In the writings of some of the early Christians we catch glimpses of what must frequently have happened. Not surprisingly, they inveighed against the Circus, convinced that it was the devil's playground, although they were even more critical of the gladiatorial games taking place in the Colosseum. The Circus Maximus stood for centuries, but its stone was eventually broken up for use in Christian buildings in the Middle Ages.

Right: Model of the Circus Maximus as it would have been in early Roman times

Below: The temple of Fortuna

The Temples of Hercules and Fortuna

Situated across the Lungotevere Aventino from the Ponte Palatino on one side and the Piazza Bocca Verita on the other, are the two small and well preserved temples of Fortuna and Hercules, both of which date from the second century BC. The rectangular temple of Fortuna was originally dedicated to Portunus, the god of rivers and ports. The temple of Hercules is often referred to as the temple of Vesta on account of its similarity to the one in the Forum.

The Jewish Quarter

The Jewish community in Rome fits well with the theme of persecution and martyrdom. It has a long history which dates back to the second century BC when Jewish merchants from Alexandria established a trading centre in the city. The book of Acts recorded the presence of Jews from Rome at Jerusalem

Right: The church of Sant' Angelo in Pescheria where Rome's Jews were forced to attend under the orders of Pope Paul IV in the mid sixteenth century

on the day of Pentecost (Acts 2:10). Their presence in the city was considerably increased when Titus, the general of the Roman army which crushed the Jewish uprising in Judea in AD 70, brought ninety-seven thousand captives to Rome. From this time onward the Jewish community in Rome grew steadily. It was further augmented in the later Middle Ages by the expulsion of the Jews from Spain, Portugal and southern Italy after 1492.

During the Middle Ages, most Jews lived in Trastevere, across the river Tiber. In 1556 this became the ghetto of Rome when Pope Paul IV ordered all the Jews in Rome to crowd into a small, walled, riverside area at the foot of the Capitoline hill where the gates were closed at night and it was hard to get out. Paul IV raised the taxes paid by the Jews and banned them from practicing any art or profession. Those who lived in the ghetto area were only allowed out during the day, and on Sundays they were forced to attend the services at the church of Sant' Angelo in Pescheria. The oppressed Jewish community was not finally freed from these constraints until 1870, when the Pope's authority in Rome was displaced by the new Italian state. The recently established authorities then decided to knock down much of the old ghetto and replace its crowded narrow streets and alleyways with apartment houses and a giant synagogue which was built in 1874.

Moving away from the Tiber side of the Ghetto, there are a number of cobbled streets, small squares, Roman remains, Renaissance palaces and Baroque churches that make this area of Rome a delight to explore. Of particular interest is the Tortoise Fountain which was designed by Giacomo della Porta as a focal point for their Piazza Mattei, and depicts four young men helping tortoises find

Above Left: *The Jewish Synagogue which stands beside the Tiber in Trastevere*

Left: *The Tortoise Fountain*

their way into a large bowl. It typifies the charm and opulence of Renaissance Rome.

The Pantheon

Pantheon means literally 'all the gods'. When the Romans took over the Greek empire, they adopted many of the Greek gods to some of whom, as we have already seen in chapter two, they gave Roman names. The Pantheon was designed in 27 BC by Marcus Agrippa, who was Consul to the Roman emperor Augustus, and completed two years later. This can be seen by reading the inscription on the lintel above the great doors: 'Built by Marcus Agrippa when Consul for the third time'. Following the Greek practice, the temple was dedicated to the deified ruler and the gods of the empire who were seen as his associates, in this case Augustus together with Mars and Venus.

Above: The Latin inscription 'Built by Marcus Agrippa when Consul for the third time' on the lintel of Portico of the Pantheon

Inset: Column detail of the Pantheon

Below: The side of the Pantheon

Above: The interior of the Pantheon

The building suffered considerable destruction by fire in AD 110 and was restored and rebuilt by the Emperor Hadrian. The Pantheon is a remarkable and awe-inspiring building. There is a huge rectangular entrance porch with granite columns behind which is a wide circular chamber (rotunda) capped with a massive rectangular dome. The building's height of 43 meters is exactly equal to its diameter. There are no windows in the Pantheon and the only light is provided by a circular opening (oculus) in the top of the dome. In wet weather the rain pours through this centre opening and runs away through drains in the floor of the building.

The Romans were remarkable builders, and they made use of concrete in the building of the Pantheon's dome. Because concrete is naturally heavy, they mixed it with pumice and allowed it to set in a wooden frame. In order to make it lighter still they made hollowed-out square sections on the inside of the dome.

The dome is still very heavy and for this reason the supporting walls are 5.79m (19ft) thick!

The Pantheon has significance in the story of early Christianity. Every religion in the Roman empire had to be licensed. It was then designated a 'religio licita' or licensed religion. With this, the registered deities could have their statues erected in the Pantheon either on small pedestals or in the niches in the walls of the building. Judaism was a licensed religion and was tolerated even though it had no images, but the early Christian church did not seek licensed status probably because they believed Jesus to be unique, the 'King of Kings', and they therefore did not want any image of him to stand alongside other Roman deities. It is interesting to reflect on the fact that the apostles Peter and Paul, who were both church leaders in Rome, must have passed by the

Right: Portrait of Raffaelo Sanzio (Raphael) 1483–1520. Ufffizi Gallery

Below: The interior of the Pantheon

Pantheon many times. With the 'Christianising' of the Empire in the seventh century, the emperor Phocas gave Pope Boniface IV permission to convert the building into a church. All the images to the gods of the Roman empire were eventually removed and the only deity subsequently to be honoured is Jesus. It has been suggested by a number of writers that the third century veneration of the Virgin Mary, the mother of God, was simply a replacement of the earlier pagan Roman worship of the Egyptian sun goddess Isis who was believed to be 'the divine mother of ancient Egypt'.

Opposite the temple entrance is a small sanctuary and choir. The wall enshrines a thirteenth century Byzantine Madonna. After the choir, beyond one more chapel and a statue of Mary, the visitor comes to the tomb of

Raphael (1483–1520), the Italian Renaissance painter whose real name was Raffaello Sanzio. In 1833 the tomb was opened up to make sure he was still there—all was well! He is buried beside his fiancée, Maria Bibbiena, who died before they could be married. Next is the monument to King Umberto, the son of Victor Emmanuel and king from 1878 until his death, and his wife, Margherita of Savoy. Finally, there is the chapel known as St Joseph of the Holy Land. The explanation which is given for this title is that a sixteenth century church official who restored the chapel packed the floor with earth from Palestine.

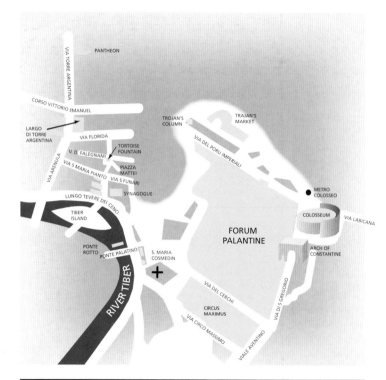

MAP DETAILING THE ROUTE FROM THE COLOSSEUM THROUGH THE CIRCUS MAXIMUS, TIBER ISLAND AND THE JEWISH QUARTER TO THE PANTHEON.

TRAVEL INFORMATION

Begin at Colosseo Metro station on line B where there are toilets to be found for a small cost. Immediately outside the main entrance there is a reasonably priced coffee shop. There are also toilets to be found on the other side of the Colosseum from the Metro and there are a number of coffee shops and affordable restaurants close by, if you climb up the steps behind the

station a few yards to the right as you exit.

After visiting the **Colosseum** and **Constantine's Arch** which stands beside it, walk down Via di St Gregorio to the end and you will come to the **Circus Maximus** on your right. Proceed to the far end of the circus and continue down hill on the Via dei Cerchi to the **Piazza Bocca Verita** where the temples of Fortune and Hercules are situated. After this,

go up the steps to the embankment and turning right and cross over the river on the Ponte Palatino, noting the remains of the **Ponte Rotto** (a broken second century BC bridge), and walk the short distance until reaching the Ponte Cestio. Walk over the bridge onto Tiber Island.

On **Tiber Island** there is an excellent ice cream shop! Once you have been served, you can sit in the piazza outside the tenth century

Left: Tiber Island

church of St Bartholomew which was built on the ruins of the **Temple of Aesculapius**, the god of healing. Significantly there is still a hospital on the island. After this brief stop, cross the **Ponte Fabrico**, the oldest working bridge in Rome, built in 62 BC, into the Jewish quarter. Follow the mini street guide through the **Jewish quarter** to the **Pantheon.**

When you reach the Pantheon enter through the main entrance and turn right, you will come to three chapels. The first one has a picture of the Annunciation attributed to an early Renaissance painter, Melozzo da Forli (1483–1498). The next contains the coffin of King Victor Emmanuel II (1820–1878), the King who united Italy in 1861 and whose great white

monument on the edge of the Forum dominates the city. The third chapel has a fifteenth century painting which represents Mary between John the Baptist and St Francis.

Below: Rome's oldest bridge Ponte Fabricio which connects Tiber Island to the Jewish Quarter

➍ The Vatican—the world's smallest nation state

The place where the apostle Peter is thought to be buried eventually became the residence of the popes, who ruled over the Roman church and much of the surrounding countryside

In addition to St Peter's Basilica and Vatican Square visitors from all over the world are drawn to the Vatican Museums, the Sistine Chapel and the Raphael Rooms. The Vatican Museums contain one of the largest collections of embroidery, painting, sculpture and other forms of fine art in the world. The buildings are also of particular interest. Some of them were designed by Donato Bramante (1444–1514) and other famous architects. It takes approximately five hours simply to walk round all the various rooms and galleries at a reasonable pace. For most people two to two and a half hours is probably the absolute maximum. Therefore it might be wise to take a break in the middle for a cup of tea or coffee or sit-down in the courtyard. When you enter the museums you will find that there are various colour-coded routes. The shortest is about ninety minutes.

A visit to the Sistine Chapel is the last port of call before you exit the museums. When you begin to feel you have had enough, it is probably the moment to start walking without stopping and follow the signs to the Sistine Chapel.

Look at a plan of the museums and choose one or two things which appeal to you. The important thing is not to try and do too much! Below are a few suggestions to note and to visit.

Maps. Almost immediately you enter the museums you will be walking down corridors which are covered with beautifully painted

Above: Maps of the papal territories in the corridors of the Vatican Museums

Facing page: A view of Vatican Square and St Peter's Basilica

maps. From this you will realise that many of the popes were a great deal more interested in land and their papal territories than in higher spiritual matters.

Bronze Pine Cone. After passing through the corridors you will see a courtyard in which there stands the famous Bronze Pine Cone. At one time it stood near the entrance to St Peter's and, according to one tradition, it was originally affixed to the Emperor Hadrian's tomb. The courtyard is a good place to get a photograph of St Peter's.

The Raphael Rooms

These were originally the apartments of Julius II who was Pope from 1503–1513. He was very impressed by Raphael's painting and chose him to decorate the four rooms. Raphael began the work in 1508 and it took sixteen years to finish. The Hall of Constantine focuses on the triumph of the Christian faith over the Roman Empire. *The Battle of Milvian Bridge* illustrates Constantine's vision of Christ and his famous victory over Maxentius in AD 312. The Room of Heliodorus depicts the protection of the church, its ministers, doctrines and property. The painting entitled *The Mass at Bolsena* shows a miracle that was supposed to have happened during a mass in 1263.

The Liberation of Peter depicts the apostle's dramatic escape from prison (Acts 12:1–19). The Room of the Segnatura contains Raphael's fresco *The Dispute over the Holy Sacrament* where a group of scholars consider the

Top: The Bronze Pine Cone which was part of an ancient Roman Fountain

Above: St Peter's Basilica from the Vatican Courtyard

meaning of the Mass. *The School of Athens* shows a debate in search of the truth between the Greek philosophers Plato and Aristotle.

The Pio Christian Museum. This is one of the Vatican's smaller museums and was founded by Pope Pius IX in the later part of the nineteenth century. It houses inscriptions and sculpture from the catacombs and early Christian places of worship. There is a fourth century statue of the Good Shepherd.

The Pinacoteca. This contains many important works by Renaissance painters including Leonardo da Vinci, Titian, Caravaggio and Raphael

The Sistine Chapel.

The Sistine Chapel (*Capella Sistina*), where the popes are elected by the cardinals of the Roman Catholic Church, is named after its founder Pope Sixtus IV. Here Some of the best painters of his day were employed to decorate the chapel and its two side walls are covered with

Above: A detail from the Battle of Milvian Bridge—School of Raphael in the Vatican Museum

paintings from the life of Christ and Moses. These were executed by Michelangelo, Perugino and Botticelli between 1481 and 1483. Of particular interest are Botticelli's *Temptations of Christ*, Perugino's *Handing over the keys of St Peter* and Roselli's *Crossing the Red Sea*. Michelangelo (1475–1564) frescoed the ceiling with scenes from the Old Testament. He completed this single-handed between 1508 and 1512, working on a specially constructed

Right: The Dispute over the Holy Sacrament by Raphael in the Vatican Museum

Above: The Good Shepherd in the Vatican Museum

Below: The ceiling of the Sistine Chapel

scaffold. Over the altar is his most famous masterpiece, *The Last Judgement*; this was also completed without assistance in 1541, after seven years of labour. In order for him to begin this work, two windows above the altar had to be removed and earlier frescoes were erased. In the picture, Jesus is portrayed in the way the medieval church regarded him as the stern Judge with little sympathy or compassion for the lost.

Simon Peter—St Peter's Basilica

Peter's original name was Simon (Acts 15:14) and his father's name was Jonah (Matthew 16:17). According to John 1:44 he came from Bethsaida but he also had a home at Capernaum in Galilee (Mark 1:21 and 30). It is possible that he may have been attracted by John the Baptist's teaching since his brother Andrew was one of the prophet's disciples (John 1:35 and 40). It was through Andrew that Peter became a follower of Jesus (John 1:41) and responded to his call to service

Above: Michelangelo's Last Judgement

on the shore of Galilee. A further call to become one of the twelve followed a short time later (Mark 3:16).

Before the day of Pentecost, Peter took the lead in the community (Acts 1:15 onward) but in the period immediately afterwards he appears more in the role of main speaker and spokesperson to the Jewish authorities (Acts 2:14 and 3:12). He was also instrumental in praying for the Holy Spirit to come on the first Gentiles in the house of Cornelius (Acts 10). There are references to his being at Joppa and then at Jerusalem where he miraculously escaped from prison (Acts 12:1–19). Peter subsequently found his way to Antioch (Galatians 2:11–14) and then at some point he arrived in Rome and it is very likely that he wrote his first letter from there. In 1 Peter 5:13 Peter wrote that 'she who is in Babylon (a well-known symbol for Rome) greets you'. Clement of Rome in his letter to the Corinthians written somewhere between AD 80 and 98, speaks of Peter's martyrdom in Rome. Stone tablets found under St Peter's Church show that Peter's memory was already venerated by about AD 120.

Caligula's Circus

The Emperor Caligula built a circus for Roman games at the foot of Vatican Hill across much of what is now Vatican Square. During the reign of the Emperor Nero, many Christians were taken to this place and thrown to wild beasts, while others were nailed to planks in the form of a cross or daubed with pitch and lighted as live torches. The remains of many of these Christian martyrs were buried on the slopes of the Vatican hill where there was already a burial ground. During recent excavations, it was observed that all the tombs converge towards one specific tomb around which there was a third century red brick wall on

Peter and 'the Rock'

Perhaps the most important event in Peter's life took place at Caesarea Philippi when Jesus asked his disciples: 'Who do people say the Son of Man is?' (Matthew 16:18). Peter immediately responded, 'You are the Christ, the son of the living God.' Jesus replied,

Above: *Statue of the apostle Peter outside St Peter's Basilica*

'Blessed are you, Simon son of Jonah … I tell you that you are Peter, and on this rock I will build my Church and the gates of Hades will not overcome it. I will give you the keys of the kingdom of heaven; whatever you bind on earth will be bound in heaven; whatever you loose on earth will be loosed in heaven.'

Interpretations of this passage have divided Roman Catholicism from Protestantism. The Roman Catholic Church takes it to mean that Peter and his successors (the popes) are the very foundation of the true church, whereas the Protestant churches understand the rock to refer either to Peter's confession or to Christ and his teaching. Certainly in the New Testament Peter is afforded no place of primacy in the church:

Jesus rebukes him (Matthew 16:23). Peter was accountable to the church at Jerusalem (Acts 11:1–18). Paul corrects him publicly (Galatians 2:11–14) and the apostles are jointly the foundation of the church (Ephesians 2:20). Peter is not mentioned in Acts after chapter 16.

Whilst it is certain that Jesus is addressing Peter here (the 'you' in verse 19 is singular), the 'keys of the kingdom' is the ministry of preaching and teaching the gospel of forgiveness and liberation from Satan's power, and this is the task of all the apostles and the whole church (Matthew 18:18; John 20:23). Nothing in the whole of the New Testament limits the leadership of the Christian church to Peter and his supposed successors.

which the letters 'PETR' have been scratched. Many believe this to be the resting place of Peter.

The Church of St Peter

In 312 Constantine became sole Emperor. He granted Christians full freedom and, to establish friendship with them, he authorized the building of a church over Peter's tomb. To make room for it, he instructed the builders to cut into the Vatican hill, and his new structure

therefore covered over many of the tombs. The first church of St Peter was consecrated in AD 326 by Bishop Silvester and the building was finished during the reign of his son, the Emperor Constantius.

During the barbarian invasions St Peter's was frequently sacked, and during the period of the 'papal exile' from 1309–1378 it fell into a ruinous state. During this time French kings virtually controlled the Papacy and

Right: Bust of the Emperor Nero. From Capitoline Museum

Below right: Bust of the Emperor Caligula, Palatine Museum

seven popes resided in Avignon. Eventually, early in the sixteenth century, Pope Julius II had part of the old St Peter's demolished and he appointed Donato Bramante to take charge of the construction of a new church. During the next hundred years a series of men took turns to supervise the work. Among them was Michelangelo who gave 16 years to the project. It was Gian Lorenzo Bernini who was primarily responsible for the interior.

St Peter's Square

Bernini was also given the task of designing St Peter's Square as a major area where crowds could gather for special feast days and celebrations. The Square is surrounded by a double colonnade with 284 Doric columns, each of which is 13m (41ft) tall. There are 140 statues each 3m tall mostly representing saints from biblical times and early Christian martyrs and theologians.

What to focus on? As with all great buildings there is so much to take in at St Peter's, so it is probably best to concentrate on a few key things. You may therefore find it helpful to use the simple plan at the end of this chapter and focus on the following aspects. Many who come to this great basilica, and indeed so much in Rome, find the lavish altars, richly coloured mosaics and icons and statues of the popes and scholars far removed from the simple form in which we know the early followers of Jesus worshipped. That said, there is a great richness of culture, beautiful religious art and Christian history to admire and take in even for those who are not practising members of the Roman Catholic Church.

1. **The Dome.** The dome of St Peter's was designed and planned by Michelangelo, and Giacomo Della Porta completed the task. The dome is 137m (438ft) high and can be seen from every part of Rome.

2. **The Façade.** The façade is the design of Carlo Maderno and was completed in 1614 after seven

Above: St Peter's Square and fountain

year's work. On the top there are 13 statues each 5.70m tall. They are Christ the Redeemer, John the Baptist and eleven Apostles. St Peter and St Paul are at the foot of the steps.

3. The Doors. There are five doors, one for each nave. Each door has sculpted bronze figures on them. The last door on the right is the 'Holy Door', which is only opened during the Holy Year. On the first day of the Holy Year the pope ceremonially opens the Holy Door and pilgrims who come to receive the special indulgence (forgiveness) pass through it. The door represents Jesus, the author of forgiveness, who said, 'I am the gate. Whoever enters through me will be saved' (John 10:9). Holy doors which are found in many Catholic cathedrals round the world are opened once every twenty-five years. Catholics who pass through the doors after confession, communion and prayer believe they receive special blessings including release from present punishment for their sins.

4. The Centre Nave. The large black Latin letters on the gold panel which runs the whole length of the nave starting on the left at the back with *Ego rogavi pro te, o Petre, ut non deficit fide tua: et tu aliquando converses confirma fraters tuo* ('I have prayed for you, Peter that your faith may never fail; and you in turn must strengthen your brothers' Luke 22:32).

5. Bronze statue of St Peter. This is situated close to the first pier, which supports the dome. It shows Peter holding the keys, blessing God's people with his raised right hand.

6. The High Altar. Sometimes known as the 'Altar of Confession'. The reason for this is that it is in memory of those Christian martyrs who were unafraid to confess their faith in Jesus even though they knew it meant death. Jesus said, 'Whoever shall confess (acknowledge) me before man, the same I will confess before my father in heaven' (Matthew 10:32). The altar was made from a huge block of Greek marble and consecrated by Clement VIII on 26 June 1594. The present altar stands over what is believed to be Peter's burial place. Numerous other Christian martyrs lie beneath the altar area.

7. The Baldacchino. The huge canopy which stands over the altar is supported by four twisted columns each of which is 20m (64ft) high. It was designed by Giovani Bernini and took nine years from 1624 to complete. The columns are decorated with olive branches and bay leaves. At the top there are several graceful cherubs. One of them carries a 'ciborium', a container for the bread of the mass.

8. The inside of the Dome. Around the base of the dome are the words from St Matthew's Gospel 16:18, 'You are Peter and on this rock I will build my Church, to you I will give the Keys of the Kingdom.'

9. The statues of Longinus, Helen, Veronica and Andrew. These four enormous statues, each nearly 10m (32ft) high, are on the inside of the four great piers, which support the dome. Each one faces inwards to the altar. Longinus is said to be the soldier who pierced Jesus' side with a spear. Helen is the mother of Constantine and the founder of Christian pilgrimage; as noted earlier she is also supposed to have discovered fragments of Jesus' cross and brought them to Rome along with the stairs leading up to Pilate's Judgement Hall. Veronica is identified in the apocryphal *Acts of Pilate* as the woman who touched the hem of Christ's garment (Matthew 9:20). According to early tradition, she wiped Jesus' face with a towel as he hung on the cross. Andrew, the brother of Peter, is thought to have taken the gospel to Greece.

Now return to the entrance on

Top: *The nave of St Peter's*

Above: *The nave ceiling of St Peter's*

the right by the main doors and start with:

10. The Chapel of the Pieta Here you will see the famous Pieta (Italian for pity) sculpted by Michelangelo before he was 25 years of age. Michelangelo's signature is on the band crossing Mary's breast. The statue shows a young looking Mary with the body of her son Jesus on her lap. Jesus' body is without wounds. She looks sad but also somehow at peace. The fact that Mary shows no sign of having aged has been seen by some as a reminder of

Left: Statue of St Peter, which over the centuries tens of thousands of pilgrims have touched or kissed as part of their devotion

Below left: The Baldachino and High Altar

1674. The tabernacle is used for storing the consecrated bread and wine of communion.

13. The Altar of Jerome The altar is decorated with a mosaic reproduction of the famous painting *The Last Communion of St Jerome* by Zampieri Domenichino (1581–1641), an Italian artist of the Bolognese school. The fifth century Jerome is best known for his translation of the Hebrew and Greek Bible into Latin; it is known as *The Vulgate* and is the official version of the Bible for Roman Catholics.

14. The Altar of Basil the Great Basil the Great (c 330–379) was Bishop of Caesarea and an able theologian. He helped the church in the fourth century to develop its teaching about the Trinity—the one God in three distinct persons: Father, Son and Holy Spirit. Basil is generally regarded as the father of Western monasticism.

15. The Altar of Wenceslas Wenceslas (d. 929), the good King of Bohemia who 'looked out on the feast of Stephen', spread Christianity in Bohemia but was murdered by his brother, Boleslav. Beside the altar are two oval portraits of Cyril (826–869) and Methodius (c 815–885) who took the Christian gospel into Eastern Europe.

16. The Altar of the Chair

the perfection of the resurrection body.

11. Monument to Pius XI Pope Pius XI (1922–1939) was the first pope to rule over Vatican City State, which was finally recognised by the Italian government in 1929 following the 'Lateran Pact' with Mussolini who had been invited by King Victor Emmanuel III to form a government in 1922.

12. The Chapel of the Blessed Sacrament The main point of interest is the gilded bronze tabernacle designed by Bernini in

Right: Michelangelo's Pieta

Below right: The interior of the Dome

of Peter This is in the apse at the end of the basilica. It is one of Bernini's masterpieces. Peter's chair is supported by four huge figures each of which is 5m tall. The two front mitred figures are Ambrose (c 339–379) bishop of Milan, and Augustine (354–430) Bishop of Hippo, and the two at the rear are Athanasius (c 269–373) bishop of Alexandria, and John Chrysostom (c 347–407) Bishop of Constantinople. Chrysostom, whose name means 'golden mouthed' was one of the most powerful preachers of his day. They were the great theologians of the early church and are clearly represented as upholding the teaching of Peter. Above the chair are two angels holding the keys which, for the Roman church, symbolize Peter's authority.

17. The Altar of the Crucifixion of St Peter The mosaic reproduction is of the picture by Guido Reni (1575–1642) and shows Peter crucified upside down as tradition claims.

18. The Altar of the Lie, or Ananias and Sapphira The mosaic of a painting by the Italian artist, Christoforo Roncalli (1552–1626) shows the punishment of a married couple, Ananias and his wife Sapphira, who were struck dead after lying to the Holy Spirit (Acts:1–11).

19. The Altar of the Transfiguration Behind and

above the altar there is a mosaic reproduction of the masterpiece of Raphael (1483–1520). Jesus is seen in the brightness of God's glory with Moses and Elijah alongside (Mark 9:4). On the ground below are Peter, James and John. In the middle, at the foot of the picture, is a young woman kneeling; she represents the church which can receive gifts and strength from above.

20. The Monument of the Stuarts The monument was begun in 1817 and completed in 1819 with George III paying the

costs. It celebrates Prince James (1688–1766), the son of James II who was deposed from the throne of England in 1688 for having earlier become a Roman Catholic. It includes also his wife Maria Clementina and their two sons Charles, 'Bonnie Prince Charlie' the 'Young Pretender', who nearly succeeded in restoring the Stuarts to the throne in 1745, and Henry who became a bishop and cardinal. After the death of Charles, the Roman Catholic Church did not recognise Henry's claim to the throne though his Jacobite followers referred to him as Henry IX. All three died as exiles in Rome.

21. Last but not least, **climb to the top of the Dome** if you have the energy. The views over the city are spectacular.

Castel St Angelo

Walk down the famous Via Conciliazone to the papal fortress and prison which was originally the Emperor Hadrian's mausoleum and dates from AD 139.

Top: The Vatican Museums' main entrance

Above left: The Vatican Museums

Middle left: Façade of St Peter's Basilica

Left: Swiss Guards at the Vatican

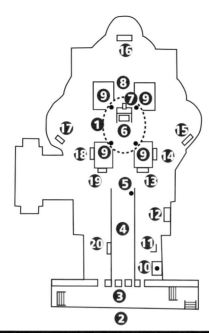

PLAN OF ST PETER'S

1 DOME
2 FACADE
3 DOORS
4 WRITING ON THE PANELS
5 STATUE OF ST. PETER
6 HIGH ALTAR
7 BALDACCHINO
8 DOME (INSIDE BASED OF DOME: 'YOU ARE PETER..')

9 STATUES
10 CHAPEL OF THE PIETA
11 MONUMENT TO PIUS XI
12 CHAPEL OF THE BLESSED SACRAMENT
13 ALTAR OF JEROME
14 ALTAR OF BASIL THE GREAT
15 ALTAR OF WENCESLAS

16 ALTAR OF THE CHAIR
17 ALTAR OF THE CRUCIFIXION OF PETER
18 ALTAR OF THE LIE
19 ALTAR OF THE TRANSFIGURATION
20 MUNUMENT TO THE STUARTS

TRAVEL INFORMATION

The Vatican Museum, St Peter's Basilica and Vatican Square are all easily reached from Ottaviano Metro. There are also a number of buses which terminate at Piazza Risorgimento which is a little closer to St Peter's. The 64 from Termini stops at St Peter's Square. Avoid eating and drinking in the Vatican as prices tend to be high. St Peter's is open 7.00am to 7.00pm (October– March closes 6.00pm). Generally the ticket office of the Vatican Museums is open from 9.00am to 4.00pm. The Museum closes at 6.00pm.

Opening times can however be quite irregular so it is worth checking on their website help.musei@scv.va or ☎ 06 6988 3333 preceded by the appropriate international code.

St Peter's is closed to the public on Wednesday mornings for a papal mass. The basilica is also closed when there are special services. It is advisable to check beforehand by contacting stpetersbasilica@gmail. com

❺ A day in Lateran

The Lateran area of the city takes its name from the
Laterani family who once owned much of the land. It
provides rich insights into both early Christian worship at
San Clemente ('one of Rome's gems') and the lavishness
and splendour which soon followed

At some point after his
conversion to Christianity
in AD 312, Emperor
Constantine confiscated land
belonging to the Laterani family.
On this he allowed the Christians
who were led by Bishop
Melchiades to construct Rome's
first official church building.

St John Lateran (San Giovani Laterano)

The present structure still bears
traces of the original design
although it has been destroyed
by fire and rebuilt on several
occasions during its history. The
architect Francesco Borromini
designed and carried out the last
major restoration of the interior
in 1646. The main facade dates
from the eighteenth century
and carries the title: 'Most Holy
Lateran Church, of all churches
of the city and the world, mother
and head.' It is the Cathedral of
Rome where, since Constantine's
time, the bishops (later popes) of
Rome have been allowed to set up
their episcopal chair (*cathedra* is
Latin for 'chair'). The church was
originally dedicated to Christ as
Saviour but with the passing of
time its name changed in keeping
with its famous baptistery which
was dedicated to John the Baptist.
It now applies to both John the
Baptist and John the Evangelist.
Until 1870 all popes were crowned
here. The pope still celebrates
mass here every Maunday
Thursday.

The Cathedral is best entered
through the main front entrance
rather than through the side
entrance which is in the Piazza
San Giovanni Laterano. The
church looks down over a
place where a number of roads
converge into the Piazza San
Giovanni, on the far side of which
stands the impressive statue

Above: *The façade of St John Lateran*

Facing page: *Piazza San Giovani with
cathedral and obelisk*

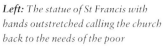

of St Francis (1182–1226) with some of his disciples. His hands are outstretched towards the Lateran. This harks back to a time when the poor man from Assisi (Francis) sought recognition for his new religious order of friars which he had founded in 1209. It is said that Pope Innocent III had a dream in which he recognised that Francis had been sent by God to recall the church away from power and wealth to a greater simplicity of life. On top of the facade are the figures of Jesus, John the Baptist and John the Evangelist with other apostles and saints.

The narthex (porch) is entered through a great bronze door which originally came from the Senate House in the Forum. At one end there is a restored fourth century statue of Constantine which was excavated from the Baths of Diocletian. To the right, the last door is the Holy Door which is walled in and only opened up during special years of Jubilee.

The nave or central part of the church is imposing with its decorative flooring, coffered ceiling, solid and impressive statues of the apostles and the papal altar under a baldachino (canopy) in the distance. Beyond that is the great apse mosaic. The coffered ceiling contains the arms of the eighteenth century Pope Pius VI. Each of the giant apostles sculpted by the Bernini School have their identifying symbols. For example, Bartholomew stands with his flayed skin and Matthew the tax

collector holds a bag of coins.
James-the-Great, the son of
Zebedee and killed by Herod
in AD 44, holds a pastoral staff
as a symbol of pilgrimage. This
is because a seventh century
tradition asserted that James
preached the gospel in Spain;
in medieval times a shrine was
erected in his honour at Santiago
de Compostela, though there
is no evidence that his remains
were ever taken there. James-
the-less (Mark 15:40), the son of
Alphaeus, was said to have been
martyred in AD 62 in Jerusalem;
it is sometimes claimed that
he was the same as the Lord's
brother who became the leader
of the church in Jerusalem, but
many New Testament scholars
believe that he didn't accept
the authority of Jesus until
he appeared to him after his
resurrection (1 Corinthians 15:7).
Thomas holds a sextant, Andrew
an X-shaped cross, Peter holds the
keys, Paul has a staff and a Bible,
and Thaddeus (Matt 10:3 and
the Judas of John 14:22) holds a
spear.

Above: *Coffered ceiling of St John Lateran*

Below: *A sketch of the original façade of St John's as it was when Bishop (Pope) Silvester consecrated the building in AD 318. The present façade was built over it and exactly matches it*

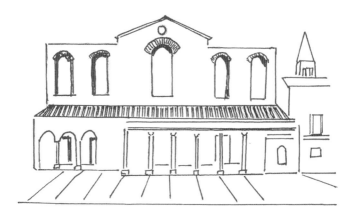

Above: *Bernini's St Paul*

The nave has five aisles in which there are one or two points of interest. Behind the first pilaster (a rectangular column) on the right as you enter the building there is a fresco by the Florentine artist, Giotto. It shows Pope Boniface VIII proclaiming the first Holy Year in 1300. Notice his crown has only one tiara (tier). In early days popes wore a one-tiered crown to indicate their rule over papal territories. Later two other tiers were added indicating spiritual power over the church and moral power over all other monarchs. Across the nave is the Corsini Chapel built by Clement XII as a mausoleum for himself and his family.

The tomb of Pope Martin V stands before the altar. The bronze work is by Simon Ghini who was a disciple of Donatello. Martin V who died in 1431 was elected by the Council of Constance in 1417 which brought to an end the papal schism which had divided the church with two rival popes both claiming authority. The inscription on the base of the coffin describes Martin as *temporum suorum felicitas* ('the joy of his times').

The high altar is covered by a heavy-looking bronze baldachino (canopy) which was designed by Giovanni di Stefano around 1370. The bronze pillars were taken from the temple of Jupiter. Below is a great relic chamber which is said to contain the heads of both Peter and Paul.

The apse mosaic was designed by two Franciscan friars, Jacopo da Torriti and Jacopo da Camerino who left their mark on the work by including themselves kneeling among the apostles. Above the gemmed crucifix is the Holy Spirit as a dove, from whose beak water flows down the sides of the cross dividing into four streams representing the fourfold gospel of the life-giving word of Christ and finally entering the broad flowing Jordan. The symbolism of all this is baptism with water and the Holy Spirit. The upper part of the mosaic depicts the head of Christ surrounded by seraphim.

The transept was designed in the sixteenth century by Jacopo della Porta and is rich in its decoration. The altar incorporates marble and bronze columns which are said to have been taken from the Temple of Jupiter in the Capitol. To the right of the Blessed Sacrament altar there is a monument to Pope Leo XIII who published an open letter to all bishops entitled

Right: Bernini's St Peter

Rerum Novarum (Latin for 'New Things'). It urged all Catholic churches to be active in bringing justice to the poor.

The cloister, which is remarkable for its twisted columns and mosaics, is entered through the transept at the end of the left aisle.

The Cathedral code

Apse: a semicircular recess at the east end of a church building where the altar is situated.

altar: a stone table for the bread and wine used in the Lord's Supper or Holy Communion.

Above: The papal chair St John Lateran

baldachino: a canopy which stands over the altar to remind people that it is a holy place.

baptistery: a pool in which people (usually adults) are immersed as a means of declaring their faith in Christ.

cloisters: are covered walkways where monks studied at desks.

confessionals: are small cubicles where people can kneel and make a private confession of their sins to a priest.

crypt: an underground chamber used for burials and sometimes for worship.

façade: (from the French meaning 'face'). The decorative outside, usually of the front, of a church.

icon: a picture or an image usually of Christ or a Saint.

narthex: an entrance porch or lobby area of a church.

nave: (from the Latin *navis* meaning a ship). The main central area of a church where the congregation gathers for worship.

sacristry: a room where the vestments worn by priests and clergy are kept.

reliquary: a room or area where relics such as bones or pieces of clothing are kept.

tabernacle: (literally a tent). A small box or locked cabinet on the altar where a portion of bread and wine from the Mass or Communion is kept.

transept: the parts of a cross-shaped church that runs at right angles to the nave.

Left: Outside the Baptistery of St John Lateran

Left: Outside the Baptistery of St John Lateran

Below: The Baptistery of St John Lateran

Piazza San Giovanni Laterano

If you leave the cathedral through the transept door, over which there is a collection of sculptured musical instruments representing King David's genius for psalmody, you come into the Piazza San Giovanni Laterano. In the middle stands a great Egyptian obelisk which dates from 1,500 BC and stood originally in front of the Temple of the Sun in Heliopolis where Moses must have seen it. Pope Sixtus V found it in a swamp in 1588 and had it brought to Rome. The inscription at the base records the baptism of Constantine.

The octagonal baptistery and its adjoining chapels are to the left as you come out of the main building into the Lateran Piazza. It dates from AD 423 and replaced an earlier construction which would have been in place since Constantine's time and in which most Christians would have been baptized by total immersion under the water, which was the practice of the earliest Christian churches.

Like many early baptisteries it is located outside the main church building. This was to indicate that there was a divide between pagan and Christian society and to symbolise that baptism was both a public witness and the means of entry into the Christian community.

The paintings around the baptistery walls depict various scenes relating to Constantine's conversion and his victory at the battle of Milvian Bridge in AD 312. See page 26. They include his vision of the cross in the sky

The papal schism

During the barbarian invasions Rome was frequently sacked and the popes were then forced to go into exile for varying periods of time. The situation was made worse in 1303 when the reigning Pope, Boniface VIII, was kidnapped by the mercenaries of King Philip the Fair of France although he eventually managed to return to Rome where he died. However, the imperial city was far from secure and his immediate successor, Benedict XI, was forced to leave it during the following year. Several of those who took office after him were French and preferred to reside at Avignon where they could count on the King's protection. Eventually however in 1378 Gregory XI was able to return and take up residence in Rome. These seventy-three years, from 1304 to 1377, are known as 'the Babylonian Captivity of the Church'. A worse calamity was to come in 1378 when there were two rival popes, one in Rome and the other back in Avignon supported by France as well as Scotland and southern Italy. The dispute was caused when the cardinals who met in the Vatican were persuaded against their will to elect an Italian pope whom they disliked. The majority of their number then withdrew from the city and elected a Frenchman, Robert of Geneva, who re-established the papal headquarters at Avignon where he felt more secure. From this point on there were rival popes in Rome and Avignon until the Council of Constance was summoned under the auspices of the Holy Roman Emperor on 1 November 1414. They ignored the rivals and chose a new pope who took the title Martin V. The period from 1378 to 1414 is generally referred to as 'the Papal Schism'.

and the Chi Rho on the soldiers' shields. The picture showing the documents burning represents the condemnation at the Council of Nicaea in AD 325 of the views of Arius, a priest from Alexandria who denied that Jesus was fully God.

The Scala Santa and Sancta Sanctorum

When the Emperor Constantine moved away from Rome to take up residence in Constantinople (Byzantium), he gave the palace of his second wife, Fausta, to the bishops of Rome to use as their residence. For almost 1,000 years the Lateran Palace which stood next to the Cathedral was the official residence of the popes. In 1304 the popes left Rome and resided in Avignon and in that same year the building was severely damaged by fire. When the popes returned from their 'Babylonian Captivity' seventy-three years later, they took up residence in the Vatican which offered greater comfort and could be more easily defended. This left the old decaying palace without a proper role, and eventually what remained was demolished during one of Sixtus V's planning and construction schemes. It was subsequently replaced by the present Lateran Palace which was rebuilt by Domenico Fontana in 1589. It was also intended to be a papal residence but was never used for this purpose.

Above: The Holy Stairs, Piazza San Giovanni

Fontana's building includes two significant remains from the old Lateran Palace, the Scala Santa (Holy Stairs) and the Sancta Sanctorum (Holy of Holies) or Chapel of St Lawrence. According to tradition, the Holy Stairs, which were the main ceremonial staircase in the old Lateran Palace, were the very stairs which Jesus ascended to Pilate's palace in Jerusalem (John 18:28). Sources in the seventh century record that shortly after her conversion to Christ, Helena the mother of the Emperor Constantine, journeyed to the Holy Land and had the stairs shipped back to Rome. They consist of twenty-eight marble steps which today are encased with wood to protect them.

The Scala Santa leads to the Chapel of St Lawrence, or Sancta Sanctorum; this was the private chapel of the popes and dates from Constantine's time although it was remodelled by Nicholas III in the thirteenth century. In the twelfth century it was decorated by the Cosmati family who developed a colourful style of mosaic decoration which has since become known as 'Cosmatesque'. The chapel is important because it was the relic treasury and still contains a number of ancient relics, the most important being an ancient icon of Christ known as the Acheiropoeton which means 'a picture painted without hands'. Two other points of interest are the statue of Pope Pius IX which stands at the foot of the stairs, and a piece of the wall of the banqueting hall from the ancient palace which can be seen from the road. It was incorporated into the building in 1743 and is decorated with a copy of the original mosaics.

Pius IX (Giovanni Mastai-Ferretti) is one of the most noted popes. In 1854 he proclaimed as part of official Roman Catholic teaching the doctrine of the 'Immaculate Conception' which asserts that the Virgin Mary was herself born 'without the stain of original sin'. In 1869–70 he convened the Vatican Council which also pronounced the doctrine of 'papal infallibility', meaning that when the pope speaks from the chair of St Peter he cannot err. Pius refused to recognise the new kingdom of Italy and retired to the Vatican in 1870 when Italian troops who had taken control over the papal lands conquered Rome and made the city the nation's capital.

San Clemente

San Clemente is one of the most remarkable buildings in the city of Rome and provides us with a real glimpse into the early church of New Testament times. It is named after Clement, the third successor to Peter as Bishop of Rome and who died about AD 100. There is very little information about this Clement though some of the second century Christian leaders knew of him. Irenaeus of Lyons (AD 180) asserted that he was a contemporary of the apostles Peter and Paul (see Philippians 4:3). Jerome wrote in 392 that a new church in Rome is dedicated to Pope Clement, a contemporary of the Roman Consul Clement. See Box on Clement of Rome page 9.

San Clemente is really three buildings all on top of each other. The reason for this is the Roman practice of taking off the upper floors of old buildings and using the rubble to fill up the ground floor. They then constructed a

new building on top of the old one. At street level there is the twelfth century church of San Clemente.

Underneath is a fourth century church and below that is a first century house church which some scholars have suggested belonged

Above: Section of the wall, from the banqueting hall of the old papal palace

Below: The twelfth century church of San Clemente

to Titus Flavius Clemens, a Roman consul and cousin of the Emperor Domitian. At some point Clemens and his wife, Domitilla, became Christians and a room in their house was in all probability set aside for Christian worship. Clemens was martyred for his faith, and his wife Domitilla continued to lead the Christian community.

In 1857 archaeologists began excavating the fourth century church and cleared out all the rubble. They then put in stanchions so that it would support the eleventh century church above it. Subsequently, by the same process, they removed all the infill from the first century Roman villa. Of added interest is the fact that archaeologists have now excavated the house belonging to Clement's neighbour and discovered that he was a pagan. This is known because in one of the rooms there is a statue to Mithras the bull god.

Above: Statue of Constantine the Great in the porch of St John Lateran

The upper twelfth century church

There is an impressive twelfth century mosaic in the apse of the upper church. The foliage represents the church with its roots in the Garden of Paradise from which also the cross of Christ, the true Tree of Life, springs, while the serpent is expelled and the baptismal waters flow. The mosaic also depicts the life of the church which not only includes the saints but also ordinary people going about their everyday business. This is represented by the farm girl feeding her poultry and the shepherd who pats his dog, as well as by various birds. The dying Christ hangs on the cross with Mary and the apostle John alongside. In the top left hand corner is St Lawrence wearing vestments patterned with flames to recall his martyrdom on a gridiron.

The choir is sixth century work which was brought up from the fourth century church below. Enshrined below the high altar are supposed to be the remains of Clement (Flavius Clement, the Roman consul and martyr) and Ignatius, Bishop of Antioch who was martyred in Rome in AD 115 probably in the nearby Colosseum (see Box: Ignatius page 40). Among other things of interest are the chapel of St Cyril and Methodius who took the gospel message to the Slavs in the ninth century, the chapel of John the Baptist with a sixteenth century statue and a modern altar, and the

Above: The apse of San Clemente

Below: Catherine of Alexandria

chapel of Catherine of Alexandria who was martyred on a wheel, after which the Catherine wheel is named.

The fourth century Church

The fourth century church is reached by purchasing a ticket and going down the steps. The church was entered through the columns on the left. A local family (probably in the ninth century) commissioned some interesting paintings on the emergency wall which tell something of the legend of St Clement after whom the church is named. He is said to have been exiled to the Crimea and eventually martyred by being thrown into the Black Sea with an anchor round his neck. The legend goes on to relate that every year when there was a very low tide, Christians visited the site of his martyrdom and found a little

chapel emerging out of the waters! See Box on Clement page 9.

Below this painting is a representation of the family who commissioned it. Their son was named after the patron saint 'Puerulus Clemens' (Little

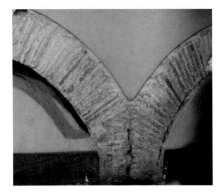

Left: Arches of the fourth century church incorporated into the wall of the twelfth century church above

Below: The sixth century choir stalls in the twelfth century church

boy Clement). A little further on is another painting which was contributed by the same family. It shows the return of the relics of St Clement to Rome. These were brought back by Cyril, 'the apostle of Russia'.

Now enter the nave between the two paintings. Round the corner on the left is a ninth century painting which is reckoned to be either the Assumption of the Virgin Mary or the Ascension of Jesus. Along the nave on the left are two more paintings. The first one tells the story of St Alexius a fourth century hermit who abandoned his wife only to discover that austerity did not suit him. He attempted to return to his wife and family who sadly failed to recognize him.

The next picture is not a very lovely story. It shows St Clement at Mass. Sissinnius, the unbelieving husband of a Christian lady, comes to scoff and is struck blind. At the right his servant leads him away.

He recovers his sight through the saint's prayers but he then spitefully orders his men to arrest Clement. However, on account of divine confusion, they lay hold instead of a column lying on the ground which they then drag away.

The House of Clement

In the far corner to the left of the altar of the fourth century church there are steps down to the 1st century house of Clement. At the bottom we find ourselves at the 'house next door'. The vault of the first room is richly decorated. The great buttresses which come down into it supports the 4th century church above. There are arches which once opened into a garden courtyard. At some point the owners made a shrine to the mysterious cult of Mithras. On either side of the little temple which resembles a cavern there

Above: Bernini's John the Apostle

are stone couches. In the centre is an altar to Mithras, a god who had an all male following and was popular among the military (see page 33). The passages now lead us through the rooms of the house of Clement till the stairs up into the forth century church are reached. Clement's house is clearly quite substantial and is built around a courtyard. This suggests that the Christian message began to impact the wealthier sections of Roman society at a fairly early point in time. It is interesting that the apostle Paul sent greetings to a number of Christian households at the end of his letter to the Romans (Romans 16:3–16).

Above: Bernini's Thomas

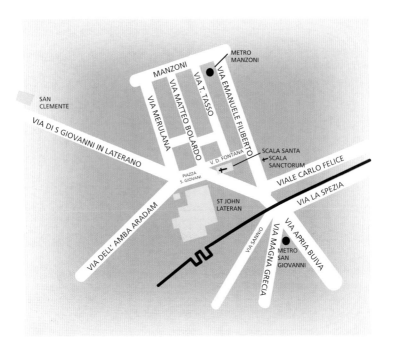

STREET MAP SHOWING ST JOHN LATERAN, THE SCALA SANTA, THE SANCTA SANCTORUM AND SAN CLEMENTE

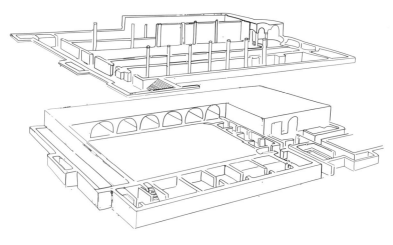

ILLUSTRATION OF SAN CLEMENTE LEVELS 1 & 2

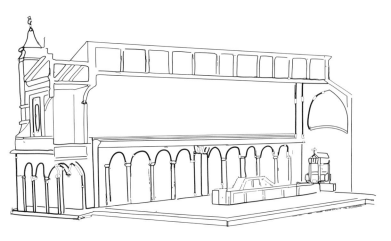

ILLUSTRATION OF SAN CLEMENTE

TRAVEL INFORMATION

The St John's website: www.catholic-hierarchy.org/diocese/dxbjl.html

San Clemente's website: www.basilicasanclemente.com

It is probably best to begin at St John Lateran (open 7.00am to 7.00pm) which is a short walk from the Metro S. Giovanni stop on line B. There are also many buses which terminate or stop at Piazza San Giovanni. The Lateran Palace and Scala Santa (which are closed from 11.50am to 3.30pm) are across the road on your left as you exit from the church's main entrance. There are toilets in the Cathedral and a variety of good cafés in the Piazza San Giovanni and in the Via Emanuele Filiberto. There is a ramp for use by disabled people at the side entrance.

San Clemente (closed 12.30 to 3.30pm) is reached by leaving the Piazza San Giovani and walking down the Via di San Giovanni in Laterano. After about fifteen minutes the Piazza San Clemente is on the right side of the road. Alternatively San Clemente can be reached by walking up the same street from the Colosseum.

Above: The courtyard and fountain outside San Clemente

❻ In the steps of the apostle Paul

The massive cobbled stones of Via Appia Antica which leads us past the catacombs of Sebastian, Callisto and Domitilla has a distinctly rural feel. This is the road on which Paul travelled to a martyr's death in the city

The Via Appia Antica (the Appian Way) dates back to 312 BC when the first section was built by Censor Appius Claudius. Further sections were built to connect Rome with the ports of Brindisi and Taranto. When the apostle Paul arrived in Italy by ship from Alexandria he was met by some of the brothers at the Forum of Appius and the three taverns. Luke relates that they encouraged him and journeyed with him to Rome, presumably along this very road (Acts 28:15–16). As the Via Antica nears the city, the Church of Domine Quo Vadis ('Lord where are you going'?) marks the spot where the Peter, who was fleeing from Rome, was said to have met the risen Christ who was entering the city and in consequence Peter was encouraged to turn back.

Under ancient Roman law no one could be buried inside the city for sanitary reasons. Many important figures were therefore buried in tombs alongside major roads, their bodies being cremated and their remains preserved in urns. As we walk down the Via Appia Antica from the junction with Via Cecilia Metella we pass several important tombs and buildings. Among them are the tomb of Cecilia Metella, the Circus of Maxentius and the tomb of Romulus. Cecilia's tomb was built between 50 and 40 BC by Marcus Crassus who was her father-in-law and one of the richest men in the Rome of his day. His son was a general in the Roman army. The private Circus of Emperor Maxentius which was built for chariot racing and dates from AD 309 is not nearly as large as the Circus Maximus but could seat 18,000 spectators. The round Pantheon-like building is the tomb of Romulus, Maxentius' much-loved son who drowned in the Tiber.

Above: The Appian Way looking down towards the Catacomb of San Sebastian

Facing page: The Appian Way with statue of the apostle Paul superimposed

The catacombs of Rome

Below: The tomb of Cecilia Metella

The catacombs are the burial places of many thousands of early Christians. As such they are a vital resource for our understanding of the life and worship of the early Christians in Rome, because although they were burial chambers, they also contained tombs of the martyrs and hence became places of pilgrimage. At least forty-six of the martyrs buried in the various catacombs are known by name. Some of the catacombs also became centres for Christian worship as the early believers gathered at the martyrs' tombs to give thanks for their lives and witness.

The catacombs of Rome also tell us about the way in which the early Christians related to Christ. They contain some of the earliest known Christian art—depictions of Jesus in particular. They also shed light on the Christians' understanding of prayer, their practice of the sacraments of Baptism and the Eucharist, as well as their strong faith in the resurrection.

The early Christians in Rome were for the most part drawn from the poorer sections of society, living in tightly packed communities along the banks of the river Tiber. Many of them were slaves, although there were some wealthy and influential members within the Christian community. Among them for example was Flavia Domitilla, a niece of the Emperor Domitian. The land under which the catacombs are situated may well have been given by rich believers such as Priscilla (the wife of the consul Acilius) or Domitilla (a member of a Roman imperial family). Even Pomponia Graecina, the wife of General Aulus Plautius who

Left: The catacomb of Callistus

conquered Britain in AD 43, was later charged with being tainted with the 'foreign superstition', which almost certainly refers to the Christian faith.

Most pagans cremated their dead, but the early Christians had a strong belief in the resurrection of the body (1Corinthians 15:42) and so did not favour the practice. Land close to the city precincts was in high demand and very expensive. This, in part, led the Christians to establish cemeteries well outside the city and to bury on many levels underground which proved to be much more economical. Contrary to popular thought, catacombs were not built as a protection from persecution, but rather as the cheaper option for burial. Nevertheless there were times when Christian groups worshipped in the secrecy of the catacombs.

One great advantage of the underground burial was the soft tufa soil. This was relatively easy to excavate and it was found that once the air got onto it, it set hard like brick and could be plastered over. The very simplest chambers in which the

Above: The avenue leading to catacomb of San Callisto

ordinary Christians were buried were plain rectangular body-sized cavities known as *Loculi*. Those Christians who were more wealthy built slightly larger chambers known as *Arcosoli* where whole families could be buried. It is on their plastered walls that most of the important paintings, prayers and memorial epitaphs are found.

From the ninth century on, the catacombs were slowly abandoned, and with the passing of the years vegetation and earth slippage covered over the entrances so that during the medieval period they were forgotten. It was not until the nineteenth century that detailed study and investigation of them really began.

The catacombs give a number of very important insights into the spirituality of the early Christians in Rome. Clearly they had a vivid experience of the personal presence of Jesus, the Good Shepherd and guide. The

Above: Pictures from the catacombs: the Eucharist together with the miracle of the feeding of the five thousand

Below: Doves of peace

emphasis seems to have been on a Jesus who transforms lives and situations: the Jesus who raises Lazarus from the grave, who touches the eyes of the blind man, who heals the woman with the issue of blood, who multiplies the loaves and changes water into wine.

The frescoes in the catacomb of Callistus in particular, indicate that Baptism and the Lord's Supper played a central part in early Christian faith, life and worship. Some of the scenes also indicate how integral the Christian faith was to everyday life. There are paintings of a farmer with sickle in one hand and vegetables in the other; a workman at the anvil and another preparing a tomb for burial. The catacombs tell us that the biblical writings were at the centre of the life of the early Christians in Rome.

The Catacomb of St Callistus

The Catacomb of St Callistus is on several levels spreading over ten kilometres. Nine third century bishops of Rome were buried in the Crypt of the Popes. In the chamber that Deacon Severus had erected for himself and his family there is a marble screen that contains the first reference to the

Right: Larger family burial chamber catacomb of Callistus

Below: Loculi in the catacomb of Callistus

bishop of Rome as 'Pope'. The Crypt of Lucina has an early third century painting showing Jesus as the Good Shepherd.

The Crypt of St Cecilia in the Catacomb of Callistus contains a replica of Maderno's statue of St Cecilia. She is shown in death making the sign of the Trinity. Cecilia founded a church in the Trastevere quarter of Rome but there is very little certain information about her except that she was an honoured martyr. Since the sixteenth century she has been regarded as the patroness of musicians and an organ is often shown as her emblem. There are several frescoes on the walls of this crypt, among which is one depicting the head and shoulders of Christ

Paul, Peter and the fire of Rome

The apostle Paul probably came to Rome about the year AD 63. When he was falsely accused by the Jews of Jerusalem (see Acts 22 to 28) he asked to be tried before the emperor in Rome because he was a Roman citizen. When Paul finally arrived in the city he had to wait a further two years for judgement to be passed. During that time he seems to have been able to preach the Christian message freely. Acts 28:30–31 records him living during that time in a rented house and states that 'boldly and without hindrance he preached the kingdom of God and taught about the Lord Jesus.'

AD 64 was the year of the great Fire of Rome which many blamed on Nero (historians still debate the evidence for this), and Nero in turn blamed the Christians. In AD 67 the Emperor Nero's persecution began and Paul was martyred along with Peter. The latter, being a foreigner, was crucified, but Paul, as a Roman citizen, was beheaded with the sword. There are many frescoes, mosaics and reliefs in Rome that depict the two apostles. Peter is often represented with curly hair, generally holding a key, and Paul is usually portrayed as balding and sometimes with a scroll or a sword in his hand. The

Below: Fresco of the Good Shepherd in the Catacomb of Callistus

early Christians in Rome greatly revered their memory. Numerous medallions bearing their images have been found in the catacombs and there are also prayers to both men inscribed on the walls of many of the burial chambers.

Peter and Paul were clearly the two most influential apostles. Peter concerned himself primarily with Jewish communities in Rome; he wrote two fine letters in Greek which was the common language in his home area of Galilee. Paul was sent to the Gentiles and interpreted the Christian message to the Greek speaking world; we have thirteen

Early Christian symbols

A feature of the catacombs is their Christian symbolism. Symbols were important to early Christians since they were a means of identifying fellow believers in what was essentially a hostile and pagan culture. Some of the most notable symbols in the catacombs are the chi rho monogram, the fish, the dove, the alpha and omega and the anchor.

The chi rho monogram of Christ is formed by superimposing the first two letters of the Greek name for Christ, X (chi=c) and P (rho=r). They therefore stand for Christ. See the coin of Magnentius on page 17.

The first letter of each word in the phrase 'Jesus Christ Son of God Saviour' forms the Greek word IXTHYS (*ichthus*) which is a fish; thus the fish became a Christian symbol (see also Matthew 4:19).

The dove, which is depicted with an olive branch, is a symbol of the Holy Spirit (Luke 3:23) and the peace of Christ

The alpha and omega are the first and last letters of the Greek alphabet and they signify the Christian belief that Jesus is the beginning and end of all things (Revelation 1:8; 21:6).

The anchor (see Hebrews 6:19) is the symbol of salvation that the believer is safely anchored to Christ Significantly the cross is rarely seen perhaps because it was still used

as a punishment for slaves and foreigners.

In the catacomb of Callistus there are portrayals of Jesus as the Good Shepherd (John 10:1–18) and the Eucharistic banquet which brings together the Eucharist and the miracle of the feeding of the five thousand (John 6:47–59). Other pictorial representations include the baptism of Jesus (Matthew 4:13–17), the multiplication of the loaves (Mark 6:30–34), Moses striking the rock, Jonah and the big fish, and five saints praying with their arms outstretched. Representations of Jesus and various biblical stories are found in the catacombs of Domitilla, Priscilla and Commodilla.

Above: Sculpture of St Cecilia by Stefano Maderno in the catacomb of Callistus. See also page 13

Below: Church of St Paul-outside-the-Walls

or fourteen letters from his hand. Around AD 170 Irenaeus, a church leader at Lyons in Gaul, wrote that 'Peter and Paul were preaching at Rome laying the foundations of the church.' Significantly, Irenaeus goes on to state that after their departure: 'Mark, the disciple and interpreter of Peter did also hand down to us what had been preached by Peter.'

For around 250 years after the death of Peter and Paul, Christians had to maintain a low profile on account of the persecutions. In that period, which lasted until Constantine granted toleration in the early fourth century, they were unable to erect official buildings for worship. Nevertheless there is good evidence that the mortal remains of both apostles were preserved and venerated. According to the fourth century church historian, Eusebius, Constantine ordered churches to be built over the remains of Peter on Vatican Hill and those of Paul which lay in a cemetery near to the Ostian Way.

Sometime later, about the year AD 390, the emperor Theodosius I ordered the remains to be removed to their present location near the Ostian Way and a new church to be constructed over them. In 1823 archaeologists found a marble plaque inscribed with the words 'Paul the Apostle, Martyr'. The apostle's remains lay beneath the slab in which three holes had been drilled, evidently to enable visitors in early times to

push pieces of material through in order to touch the saint's remains and thus receive healing properties. It was this same tomb which is inscribed with the words 'Paul Apostle and Martyr' that the archaeologist, Giorgio Filippi, found during extensive excavations in 2006.

The Church of St Paul-outside-the-Walls

The church was built at the place where, according to tradition, the remains of the apostle Paul were believed to have been buried on the orders of Constantine. Again according to tradition, the first edifice that was built was consecrated by Bishop (Pope) Sylvester on 18 November 324. Several of Constantine's successors felt that a more impressive structure was called for, and emperors Valentinian II, Theodosius I and Arcadius all made contributions. The church that finally emerged was an impressive structure on a Latin cross plan with a nave and four aisles that are separated by rows each with twenty massive columns. It was consecrated in 390 by Bishop Siricius. The building remained very much as it had been at the beginning until 1823 when a huge fire destroyed a large part of the nave. The reconstructed church kept the early Christian architectural layout although many of the medieval additions were lost. The new building was consecrated by Pope Pius IX.

Some key features of the church include:

The Courtyard. The church is entered through a spacious square courtyard with 146 columns which was built between 1890 and 1928. The centre is dominated by an imposing statue of St Paul

Above: A statue of St Paul in the courtyard outside the church of St Paul-outside-the-Walls

Above: Statue of St Paul in the nave of the church of St Paul-outside-the-Walls

Paul's gospel

In his letter to the Romans Paul outlined the doctrine of justification by faith alone through the sinless death of Christ on the cross. He condemned the idea of good works or any human endeavour or ceremony making a person right with God. Faith in Christ alone was sufficient. This became the hallmark of the Protestant Reformation that in the sixteenth century spread across Europe through men like Luther (Germany), Calvin (Switzerland), Tyndale (England), Groote (Holland). It set these 'evangelical' men on a collision course with the Church of Rome which believed the church dispenses salvation through images, saints, ceremonies and priests. The result was many more martyrs but by a different persecutor.

Paul was the major influence in the development and spread of the Christian message across the Roman Empire. While on the Damascus road he had received a dramatic personal encounter with the risen Christ that completely transformed his life. Saul of Tarsus, formerly a persecutor of the Christians, became Paul the apostle, evangelist and later martyr. Most of the New Testament letters come from his hand. His letter to the Romans has been called: 'The Gospel according to Paul' and is generally acknowledged to be one of the clearest statements of the Christian message. Samuel Taylor Coleridge once described it as 'The most profound book ever written'. The apostle Paul also set out in detail the Christian doctrine of the resurrection. Additionally, Paul was a supreme church planter and strategist. During his missionary journeys into the hinterland of Asia Minor he set up congregations on the synagogue pattern with elders and deacons.

holding a sword in one hand, the symbol of his martyrdom, and the word of God in the other, emphasising his role as an evangelist and an apostle. The statue was the work of Giuseppe Obici. Paul is also depicted underneath the apex of the main façade. Christ is seated on the throne in the middle with Peter on his left and Paul on his right. Below this panel in the centre Christ is shown as the Lamb of God standing on a hill from which four springs flow to where twelve lambs drink, symbolizing the twelve apostles. The cities of Jerusalem can be seen in the background.

The Central Aisle. On the lavishly decorated ceiling of the central nave aisle, the coats-of-arms of the three popes who contributed to the rebuilding can be seen. Between the windows and bordered by Corinthian pillars there are 36 frescoes

Above: The courtyard of St Paul-outside-the-Walls

Above: The Altar of St Paul-outside-the-Walls

Below: The cloisters of St Paul-outside-the-Walls

which illustrate events in Paul's life that are found in the book of Acts. Beneath the windows of the central and side aisles are mosaic portraits of all the popes from Peter to the present time. The idea was first begun by Pope Leo the Great in the fifth century and the portraits were painted in frescoes.

The Apse. The oldest part of the building is the apse and the triumphal arch, the structures of which were unaffected by the fire. However, the original thirteenth century mosaics did suffer considerable damage and were replaced by replicas that include heads of the apostles and images of birds. At the centre of the apse Jesus is depicted sitting on a throne—flanked by Peter and Andrew on his left and Paul and Luke on his right—in a meadow in which there are flowers and animals. Kneeling at his feet and clad in white is Pope Honorius III who had commissioned the original mosaics. At the foot of the arch are two large statues of Peter and Paul on marble pedestals.

The Altar. The canopied altar (baldachino), which dates from 1285, survived the fire of 1823. It was designed by Arnolfo di Cambio. In the niches on the sides there are statues of Peter, Paul, Timothy (Paul's disciple) and Benedict, the founder of the Benedictine monastic order. The Altar of Confession was built over the tomb of the apostle. The remains of Timothy are believed to be buried close to those of the apostle.

The Cloisters. The present cloisters were built between

Right: A nineteenth century depiction of the fire at St Paul-outside-the-Walls

1208 and 1235. They played an important part in the life of the monks who lived and worked here. Today, apart from the cloisters, little remains of the ancient monastery. The fragments of both pagan and Christian tombs that are on the walls of the cloisters were found under the floor during the restoration following the great fire of 1823. Adjoining the cloisters there is a hall and a relic chapel. The latter contains a number of interesting exhibits including what are supposed to have been the prison chains of St Paul.

The Bell Tower. This is a relatively recent construction that replaced the fourteenth century bell tower. It is composed of five different levels each of which is in a different style.

Post script. The Church of San Paolo is one of Rome's four major basilicas. It is an impressive structure which, despite the great fire of 1823, still conveys the grandeur and strength of the Roman empire of the days of Constantine and Theodosius. Above all, it is a place of pilgrimage which, for many centuries, Christians have visited out of thankfulness for the inspiring life, witness and teaching of the great apostle who played such a major part in shaping the Christian faith.

TRAVEL INFORMATION

The best way to reach the Catacombs is to take the Metro line A to Coli Albani and then catch the 660 bus immediately outside to the Via Appia Antica. The Catacomb of Callisto (closed on Wednesdays) which is possibly the most interesting in terms of Christian art is open 8.30 am to 12.00 pm and 2.30 to 5.30 pm. There is a modest admission charge but very helpful and often inspirational guided tours are given. Going underground for 30 minutes is a cold experience so an extra sweater is advisable. The nearby Catacombs of San Sebastian (closed on Thursdays) and Domitilla (closed on Tuesdays) are open for the same duration as Callisto. There are toilets at Callisto and drinks and snacks can be purchased.

For the church of St Paul-outside-the-Walls the easiest way is to take the Metro line B to San Paolo. There are also several buses from the city centre including the 170 from Termini. For those travelling by car it is probably best to leave Rome on the Via Appia Nuova and turn off onto Via dell' Almone which will bring you onto the Via Cecilia Metella and the Via Appia Antica.

❼ The Forum, Palatine and Villa Borghese

The Forum and the Palatine, despite their largely ruined state, still give the feel of the grandeur and splendour of the ancient Roman Empire, while the Park and Villa Borghese reflect the opulence of their founder and patron of the arts, Cardinal Scipione Borghese

The origin of the 'Forum', or more particularly forums since there are several, goes back to the days of the Republic which was founded in 509 BC. The rulers built these forums or central squares largely for their own self-aggrandisement. It was customary to build temples in memory of the living, as for example the great temple which was built by the Senate and dedicated to the Emperor Antoninus and his wife Faustina. In the seventh century, the temple was transformed into a Christian church which is why it has survived in its present form. The pattern of all the forums was fairly similar: a large colonnaded square with a colossal statue of the ruler himself in the centre and a temple at the end. The area which runs between the Colosseum and the Emmanuel Monument, generally referred to as the Forum, in fact encompasses the forum of Julius Caesar and the forums of Emperors Augustus, Nerva and Trajan. The Forum was the heart of the ancient city. Among other buildings there were the Senate House, the temples, the law courts and the residence of the Vestal Virgins. Titus Plautus, the Roman poet, wrote that the Forum of Rome 'teemed with lawyers and litigants, bankers and brokers, shopkeepers and strumpets [prostitutes] and good-for-nothings waiting for a tip from the rich.'

The Forum
To fully appreciate the Forum the visitor really needs to stand on either the Capitoline or Palatine hills and look down on it. The Forum was the great centre of ancient Rome. Here were situated

Above: *View of the Forum from the Capitoline Hill*

Facing page: *An overview of the Forum, looking down from behind the Emmanuel Monument*

all the government buildings, the law courts, temples to the most important Roman gods and memorials and triumphal arches commemorating major victories on the part of the nation's armies. The political empire, which was controlled by the military and ruled over by the emperors, began to collapse early in the fifth century. In its place the so called 'Holy Roman Empire' gradually emerged. This was held together by the church and ruled over by the bishops of Rome (later called 'popes' from the Latin *papa*, father). During the long period of the church's dominance, which lasted almost to the nineteenth century, many of the buildings of the old political empire in the Forum fell into disrepair and most of the stones were taken away to be used in constructing new churches and other buildings. At the beginning of the eighteenth century the Forum had become a rubbish tip and dumping ground.

At that time the Arch of Septimus Severus was half buried, and much of what we see today was covered over with earth and animals were grazed on top of it. Archaeological investigations, which are still continuing, began in the eighteenth century.

At the time of the Second World War, the Forum was much larger than it now appears because Benito Mussolini constructed a major road, the Via dei Fori Imperali, through the middle to facilitate his military parades! Two things on the other side of this highway are worthy of note: Trajan's Market and Trajan's Column. Roman citizens were not a great deal different from their present day counterparts. Many of them would start the day at the gymnasium or the Baths of Caracalla or Augustus and then go into the Forum to pay their respects to the deities followed by a bit of retail therapy in the markets!

Above: *Forum from Capitoline Hill*

Right: Forum from
Capitoline Hill

Below: The Arch of Titus

Bottom: Detail from the
arch of Titus showing the
Jewish menorah being
carried in triumph after
the destruction of the
Temple. On the opposite
side there is a panel which
depicts the Emperor
Titus in triumph

As in every other part of Rome
there is much to see. You may
therefore find it helpful to use
the map in the travel section here
to concentrate attention on the
following.

The Arch of Titus

Arches were built to
commemorate the most
important victories of the Roman
empire. The Arch of Titus was
commissioned by the Senate in
celebration of the achievements
of the Emperor Titus after his
death in AD 81. The Arch and
the Colosseum have in common
the fact that they were both built
by Jewish captives who were
brought back to Rome after the
destruction of Jerusalem in AD
70, a devastation which Jesus
Christ had foretold (Luke 21:21–
24). His prophecy also asserted
that the temple would be laid
waste till not one stone remained
on another (Matthew 24:2). A
careful glance under the inside of
the Arch evidences the fulfilment
of Jesus' words in the sculptures
of the Roman soldiers carrying
away from the temple silver
trumpets and the great seven
branch candlestick or menorah.

Go through the arch or round
it and turn right down the sloping
path until you come to the Basilica
of Maxentius.

Above: Arch of Titus name stone

The Basilica of Maxentius

The word 'basilica' has no religious significance; its original meaning was 'a royal hall'. Work began on this building in the early fourth century during the brief period in which Maxentius controlled the city. Following his defeat by Constantine at the battle of Milvian Bridge in AD 312, the work continued under the new emperor. For this reason, it is sometimes called the Basilica of Constantine. The inside consists of a nave and two side aisles. The right aisle is all that remains in the current structure. The building was used as a law court and also for administrative purposes. One significance of this building is its vast size. It covers roughly 100.5m (330ft) by 65.5m (215ft) and it is 35m (115ft) high. The great arches span 22.8m (75ft). In the apse at the west end there was a statue of Maxentius which was later replaced by a statue of the Emperor Constantine 11.8m (39ft) high. The giant head and a foot of this statue are still on display at the Palazzo dei Conservatori. The roof was once covered with gilded tiles but they were stripped off in the seventh century and used to decorate the roof of St Peter's.

Continue on the main pathway till you come to

The Curia/Senate House

This was the Parliament House

Right: Basilica of Maxentius, an impressive hall and place of justice, named after the rival emperor whom Constantine defeated in AD 312

or Council Hall of Rome. The building was begun by Julius Caesar in 52 BC but, after being damaged in the fire of AD 64, was brought to its present form by the Emperor Diocletian in AD 283. The inlaid floor is perfectly preserved. The doors are copies of the originals which were pillaged by Pope Alexander VII for the church of St John Lateran. The present building was reconstructed in the early twentieth century. Inside there are two stone balustrades. The sculptures on the left represent the cancellation of debts with the tablets being brought to the Emperor Constantine for destruction. The one on the right represents the institution of the new child welfare laws. A mother with her children are pictured thanking the emperor. In the front of the Senate House is the Rostra where important speeches were delivered to the populace.

The Arch of Septimus Severus

This arch was erected in AD 203 and it recalls the victories in battle in the eastern part of the empire in Parthia (present day North East Iran) and Arabia. The more important panels are representations of the most significant victories of Septimus Severus. What appear to be angels over the arch are conventional Roman figures of victory. All the Roman emperors who came before Constantine were pagans who worshipped the Roman gods. Some, such as Septimus Severus, were particularly active in persecuting the Christians.

Top: The Curia

Above: Arch of Septimus Severus

The Julian Basilica

This huge building was begun in 54 BC by Julius Caesar and so is called the Julian Basilica. After his death it was completed by his great nephew Octavian, who took the title Augustus. It was a law court for civic trials. While people waited to have their cases heard they often played games on the pavement, and it is possible to see some of their 'gaming boards' which were cut into the stone and used for throwing dice.

The Temple of Castor and Pollux

The ruins of this temple are easily recognised by the three fluted columns supporting the fragile remains of a lintel. The temple is believed to have been dedicated to Castor and Pollux in 484 BC following the battle of Lake Regillus in which the Roman dictator, Postumious, defeated the Tarquin kings. The building was restored many times and the present remains probably date from the time of the Emperor Tiberius who rebuilt and consecrated it in AD 6 when heir to the throne. He became emperor in AD 14. Castor and Pollux were originally the Greek gods Dioscuri and Polydeuces, the twin sons of Zeus by Leda, who were believed to be the protectors of mariners. Luke tells us in Acts 28:11 that the apostle Paul set sail for Rome on an Alexandrian ship with the figurehead of the twin gods Castor and Pollux. See chapter one for details of the Greek and Roman pantheon.

The House of the Vestal Virgins

This is easily recognised by the fish ponds which are within the complex. Vesta was the goddess of light and hearth and she was worshipped in every Roman house in ancient times. In the temple of Vesta, a small part of which has been restored, was a round building supported on colonnades in which a sacred flame was kept burning day and night by six vestal virgins. They were privileged venerated women chosen by the High Priest (Pontifex Maximus) whose residence was also in the Forum. Vestal Virgins were of noble birth and were selected when they were between six and ten years old and they served for thirty years. At their initiation ceremony their hair was cut and they were clothed in white garments. The first ten years were spent learning their duties, the next ten performing them and the final ten teaching the novices. They had to remain virgins, and the punishment for disobedience was to be buried alive in the Villains' Field. History records that ten Vestals were known to have suffered this punishment. The men involved were whipped to death.

Within the complex there are a number of pedestals on which were the statues of some of the most famous high-born Vestal Virgins. On one of the pedestals the name of the

Above: *Remains of Temple of Castor and Pollux*

virgin has been removed. It has been suggested that this may have been Claudia who abandoned her position to become a Christian, although little is known of her. The annual festival of Vesta was held between 7 and 15 of June and the temple was cleaned and decorated with flowers.

Above: House and gardens of the Vestal Virgins

Below: Remains of the Temple of Vesta

Trajan's Markets

These were once considered to be one of the seven wonders of the world. The present remains give only a hint of their former glory. Between AD 100 and 112 the Emperor Trajan and his architect, Apollodorus of Damascus, designed and built this amazing complex of 150 shops and offices. The shops on the ground floor were smaller and sold mostly vegetables and fruit. The shops on the upper level are believed among other things to have sold oil and wine. There is an entrance fee to this complex and it takes at least an hour to see everything.

Trajan's Column

This tall 95m (304ft) column was commenced by Trajan in AD 113 and recounts in graphic detail his two campaigns in Dacia (Romania) in AD 101–102 and 105–106. The sculptures begin with the Romans preparing for

Above: Trajan's Market

Below: The Mamertine Prison

war and end with the Dacians being driven out of their land. The column was originally topped with a statue of Trajan but this was replaced in 1588 with a statue of St Peter. See the Box: Emperor Trajan for his view of the Christians. When Trajan died in AD 117 his ashes, along with those of his wife Plotina, were placed in a golden urn at the foot of the column.

The Mamertine Prison

The prison is situated below the church of San Guiseppe dei Falegnami (St Joseph the

Carpenter). It is made of huge blocks of stone and believed to date from 640 BC. According to one tradition—fifth century but not necessarily unreliable—the apostle Peter is said to have been imprisoned here and to have baptised two of the prison guards. *The Acts of Martyrs* relates that Hippolytus, a third century Roman bishop, was also held captive here.

The Palatine

The Palatine Hill was a favoured area where many of Rome's richest and most influential citizens had their homes. Among them were the great

Emperor Trajan

The Emperor Marcus Ulpius Nerva Trajan (53–117) was Roman Emperor from AD 98–117. He was an able military leader and strategist who extended the empire to its greatest point by winning distinguished victories in Dacia and Parthia. The Dacian King, whose territory bordered the Danube, surrendered to Trajan in AD 102 but rebelled again only to be finally put down in AD 106. As a result of these victories, Trajan took possession of Dacian mines and other resources which enabled him to embark on a number of major building projects. These included his new forum, an extensive shopping mall (Trajan's Market), his monument and the huge imperial baths on the Esquiline hill. Among other things, Trajan had an important correspondence with Pliny the Younger who was the provincial governor of Bythinia about the Christians in his area. Pliny stated that the Christians 'were accustomed to meet on a fixed day before dawn and sing responsively a hymn to Christ as to a god. So far from binding themselves by oath to commit any crime, they swore to keep from theft, robbery, adultery, breach of faith, and not to deny any trust money deposited with them when called upon to deliver it.' Pliny also went on to say that 'it was their custom to depart and to assemble again to partake of food, but ordinary food'. Trajan's response was: 'They are not to be sought out; if they are denounced and proved guilty, they are to be punished, with this reservation, that whoever denies that he is a Christian and really proves it, that is by worshiping our gods, even though he was under suspicion in the past, shall obtain pardon through repentance. But anonymously posted accusations ought to have no place in any prosecution. For this is both a dangerous kind of precedent and out of keeping with the spirit of our age.'

Above: *Trajan's Column*

orator Cicero, and Augustus who was born here and continued to live here in a fairly simple manner when he became Rome's first emperor in 28 BC. It was Augustus who sent out the decree that all the Roman empire should be taxed (Luke 2:1) which resulted in Joseph and Mary travelling to Bethlehem. His successor and step son, Tiberius, also lived on the Palatine and built himself a magnificent home, the Domus Tiberiana. Another emperor, Septimus Severus, who harshly persecuted the early Christians, also built a palace there. Most of the Palatine buildings are largely in ruins with only the remains of walls and fragments of paving and mosaic floorings still in existence. There are shaded pathways, orange groves and ornamental shrubs. Be sure to spend some time looking down on the Forum below. It's a panoramic view. The

Left: The Palatine from the Forum

following are a few key remains which are worth visiting.

The House of Augustus and the House of Livia. The first may have been an official residence and the House of Livia, the wife of Augustus, their private residence. This, of course, is the Augustus of Luke 2:1. The Roman historian, Suetonius, relates that Augustus slept in the same room in a low bed and wore plain clothes woven by Livia and his sister, Octavia. This house is particularly interesting on account of wall paintings which have survived from the first century.

The Domus Augustana was designed for the emperor, Domitian, by the architect Caius Rabirus between AD 81 and 96. It was part of his private residence. Domitian was one of several Roman emperors who believed himself to be divine and demanded the worship of all his people. Christians who refused to declare, 'Caesar is Lord', were harshly treated and many of them preferred to die rather than deny Jesus. Domitian, who had an excessive fear of assassination, was in fact murdered in a palace conspiracy.

The Palatine Stadium adjoins the Domus Augustana and is the Palatine stadium which was built by Domitian, either as a public stadium or possibly as a private track for exercising horses. The stadium was later used for foot races by Theodoric the Ostrogoth (c 424–526).

As you walk around the Palatine you will be able to look down on the Circus Maximus which lies between the Palatine and Aventine hills. Little remains of what was the largest circus in the city. The obelisks which now stand outside St John Lateran and in the Piazza del Popolo once stood in the middle of the circus. See page 45 for the Circus Maximus

The Palace of Septimus Severus

This was built by the emperor Septimus Severus. One point of interest is a specially constructed Imperial Box from which the emperor and his family and guests could watch the games and races in the circus below.

Right: Inside the House of Augustus

Below right: Villa Borghese

Villa Borghese

The Villa Borghese was designed in 1605 for Cardinal Scipione Borghese, a nephew of Pope Paul V. It was built between 1613 and 1616. The park which surrounds the villa was meticulously planned with a variety of trees and sculptures and became a pattern for a number of other later Italian stately homes. The Cardinal had the building designed to house his famous collection of mosaics, sculptures and paintings. The building was improved in the eighteenth century and there were a number of important subsequent additions. Today the Villa and Gallery belongs to the state. It houses a remarkable collection of some of Bernini's finest sculptures and a rich collection of Renaissance painting which includes works by Titian, Rubens, Raphael and Caravaggio.

The ground floor (The Museo). In the entrance hall there are some beautifully preserved fourth century mosaics of hunting scenes and gladiators fighting wild beasts. These mosaics were lifted from the floors of early Roman villas.

Room 1 Canova's celebrated sculpture of Napoleon's sister, *Pauline Borghese*. In its day it was considered scandalous since Pauline is semi-naked and posing as Venus.

Above: Cardinal Scipione Borghese, the Gallery Borghese

Room 2 Bernini's famous sculpture of *David* poised with his sling ready to hurl a stone at Goliath. Bernini was only twenty-one when he created this sculpture.

Room 3 Bernini's masterpiece, *Apollo and Daphne*. Daphne is fleeing from the sun god Apollo.

Room 4 Bernini's *Pluto and Persephone* which shows Pluto carrying off his bride. The delicate nature of the piece is almost breathtaking.

The upper floor (The Galleria)

To reach the upper floor, exit from the front entrance and walk round to the back of the building where you will find the way in and stairs. There are a number of interesting paintings by Caravaggio, Raphael and Holbein. Of particular note are Caravaggio's *John the Baptist* and *David with the Head of Goliath*.

Above: Bernini's David

Below: The Forum

Opposite page: Looking up to the Palatine from the Forum

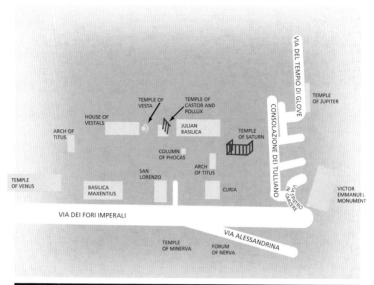

MAP OF TEMPLES IN FORUM AREA

TRAVEL INFORMATION

For the **Forum** and the **Palatine** take either the Metro or one of the many buses to the Colosseum. The entrance is beside the Arch of Constantine. There is a charge to visit both the Forum and the Palatine which can be entered either at the entrance close to Constantine's Arch or from the Forum. Further information can be found at www.italianvisits.com/tickets/palatine_hill.htm

Villa Borghese. There are eight buses which stop on the Viale Paolo del Brasile on the edge of the Park, including the small electric bus 116 which goes right into the Park. One other easy way is to take the Metro line A to Spagna. As you come up from the station platforms there is a long escalator which goes up to the edge of the park. Follow the Viale Del Museo Borghese to the Villa.

You need to book tickets in advance on line at www.ticketeria.it/ticketeria/borghese-eng.asp

It is essential to use an audio handset which will give you a short commentary on each of the important sculptures or paintings. The handset counter is located in the main entrance area. You have to collect a handset before you enter the rooms which house the collection. It costs a few euros but it is essential.

Don't try to do too much. It is far better to look at a limited number of really good things and try to appreciate them and then sit outside or enjoy a tea or a coffee rather than to attempt to do the entire collection. Visitors are allotted a specific time of only two hours duration. Further information can be obtained from the official website www.galleriaborghese.it.

⑧ A day in Pompeii

'There stands the long rows of solidly built brick houses (roofless) just as they stood eighteen hundred years ago, hot with flaming sun…and here are the Venuses, and the Bacchuses, and Adonises, making love and getting drunk in many-hued frescoes on the walls of saloon and bed chamber…and there are the bake shops, the temples, the halls of justice, the baths, the theatres, all clean scraped and neat' (Mark Twain, *Innocents Abroad*)

This chapter is added because, although Pompeii and its sister city, Herculaneum, lie some 240 kilometres from Rome, many visitors to Italy will want to visit this extraordinary archaeological exhibit. Nowhere will we find a better description of ordinary life in a Roman city at the time the first Christian churches were born.

The city of Pompeii was buried beneath the lava of Mount Vesuvius when it erupted on 29 August AD 79. Perhaps 2,000 inhabitants, less than ten percent of the population, failed to escape in time. Centuries later archaeologists found the petrified bodies of a father leading his wife and two daughters in a vain attempt to escape the suffocating fumes and the pyroclastic flow; the doctor still carrying his bag of medical instruments, a little girl clinging to her mother's dress, and the guard dog straining at its leash to break free. Bread was still in the oven, painters left their tools and paint pots in an unfinished room, and the graffiti of lovers and electioneers daubed the walls of the city.

Pompeii was connected to the capital by well-constructed roads. Its population has been estimated at about 12,000, with double that number living outside the city, perhaps half of whom were slaves. In Victorian times

Above: *Depiction of Vesuvius from the BBC programme* In the shadow of Vesuvius, *5 November 2009*

Facing page: *A street in Pompeii with Vesuvius in the background*

no grand tour of Italy would have been considered worthy of the name without a visit to Pompeii. The excavations have given us a marvellous picture of a Roman town, including such diverse aspects as water supply, sewerage, gardens and what was sold in the shops. All this provides us with a good understanding of what first century Roman society was like and in particular the challenges that were faced by any Christians who may have lived there.

Pompeii was occupied by the Romans in 310 BC but enjoyed a measure of independence until a revolt in 89 BC, as a result of which Rome imposed its own language, law and culture. The city was devastated by a major earthquake in AD 62

Christians in Pompeii?

We do not know for sure whether there were Christians among the inhabitants living in Pompeii at the time Vesuvius erupted, but it is by no means impossible. It is clear from the book of Acts that there were Christians at nearby Puteoli (Pozzuoli) which was less than twenty-five miles away. When the apostle Paul landed there on his way to Rome (Acts 28:14) he stayed with them for a week and was encouraged by them. This view is supported by the discovery during the excavations of 1925 of a Christian palindrome Rotas Sator Square found etched on the wall of the bathroom in the house of Paquius Proculus who was a Mayor of Pompeii. Also found in their home is a painting which some have taken to be of Paquius Proculus and his wife. Palindromes have been found in a

number of Roman villas and houses across the Roman empire. They are engraved tiles that appear to be a jumble of letters and have the appearance of a small word search puzzle. The letters make the Latin words 'pater noster' twice, meaning 'our Father' with the letters 'A' (Alpha) and 'O' (Omega) before and after each 'pater noster'. See Revelation 22:13 for the description of Christ as the alpha and omega, the first and last letters of the Greek alphabet. These

Above: A Rotas Sator palindrome which perhaps was a coded clue that a house or premises belonged to Christians

signs were designed to let visitors know that they had entered a Christian household. There is some evidence of a Jewish community in Pompeii although no synagogue has been located. There are one or two possibly Jewish names and a clear reference to Sodom and Gomorrah in one graffiti.

when, according to the Roman historian Tacitus: 'a large part of Pompeii collapsed.' It is evident that many of its buildings were either undergoing reconstruction or repair when the city was engulfed by red hot lava seventeen years later.

Many of the city's inhabitants had failed to heed the warnings and leave the city when molten lava began to fall on the town, since more than a thousand bodies have so far been unearthed in the excavations. It has been suggested that perhaps as many as twice that number may have lost their lives in the inferno.

The city was governed by a local council elected by the male citizens of the city. Council members had to be adult males who were respectable and wealthy free citizens. The city had the familiar contrasts between the rich who lived in spacious homes while others who were less well off had to make do with small dwellings or rooms above their shops. They were not entirely devoid of creature comforts, a fact attested by the discovery of around two hundred lavatories within the main area! A number of the wealthier homes were decorated with wall paintings, and columns bore coloured patterning. Representations of the gods and goddesses and hunting scenes were popular. We know from extant shop signs that Pompeii offered many goods and services to its people, among them banking, restaurants, bakeries, building work, lamp-making, shoe shops, jewellery and laundry.

Wealthy Pompeiians no doubt dined in style reclining on cushion covered couches and enjoyed Roman delicacies such as roasted boar and stuffed dormice! In

Below and inset: The House of the Faun is the largest house in Pompeii excavated so far

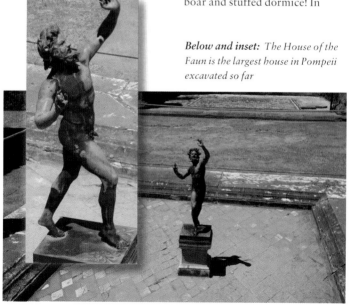

contrast, the majority of ordinary citizens, many of whom lacked cooking facilities, probably made do with bread, olives, wine, fruits and vegetables.

A visit to Pompeii

For the benefit of those who want to visit Pompeii, the city is divided into nine regional areas which are further subdivided into smaller localities. This makes it relatively easy to locate particular temples, shops and houses. Because there is far too much in Pompeii to see in one day, it is essential to be selective. The following are recommended not only as being interesting architecturally but also because of the way in which they reflect the life of the town and the impact that this would have had on Christian people. The words 'Sodom and Gomorrah', two cities in the book of Genesis on which the Lord rained down fire and brimstone, inscribed in large letters on the wall of a house on Via dell' Abbondanza, may indeed be an accurate commentary on the town's moral life as well as the catastrophic disaster it experienced. It almost certainly reflects the presence of Jews in the city, if not Christians.

The House of the Faun is the largest and most visited house in Pompeii. Named after the bronze statue of a dancing faun, it also has several detailed floor mosaics one of which depicts Alexander the Great fighting King Darius of Persia at Issus in 333 BC.

The House of the Tragic Poet takes its name from the mosaic depicting actors performing a Greek drama. Mosaics like this are an important means of helping modern historians in their understanding of ancient Roman life. This is a typical second century BC Roman house which has been the source of several works of fiction. It has some remarkably well preserved mosaics and frescoes from Greek mythology. Prominent among them is the mosaic of a chained dog with the words *Cave Canem* (beware of the dog) at the bottom. The images on the walls include Zeus and Hera, Aphrodite, Helen and Paris and Eros and Poseidon.

Villa of Mysteries is an example of a luxurious suburban house with a farm annex. The house, which is built on a steep slope looking out to sea, stands over a cellar area. It has kitchens, an oven and a servants' quarter. There are a number of wall paintings in the house which depict Dionysian ceremonies.

The Amphitheatre is one of the most impressive structures in Pompeii. Built at the behest of Quinctius Valgus and Marcus Porcius, it dates from 70 BC and had a seating capacity for 20,000 spectators. The theatre was the venue for gladiatorial combat, animal shows, hunts and other contests. Gladiators were most frequently men and often either slaves or condemned criminals. Female gladiatorial contests were however staged and proved very popular; wall reliefs, though not at Pompeii, show them in action. Each gladiatorial troupe had a manager, whose task it was to look for fresh talent in the local slave markets in much the same way that football clubs send out scouts to search for rising talent. During excavations a number of helmets came to light at Pompeii in a large open space in the vicinity of the theatre, leading to the conclusion that this was the base where gladiators lived

Below: The Mosaic of a chained dog in the House of the Tragic Poet

and trained. We know from advertisements that gladiatorial shows in Pompeii could be lengthy affairs sometimes lasting as long as five days.

The theatre was therefore the scene of much bloodshed and death as gladiators fought with one another. Also popular among the town's inhabitants were contests between men and animals, mostly bulls and bears, a fact reflected in some of the stone panels discovered in the excavations. Judging from the many images and sculptures, both large and small, that have been unearthed in the town, gladiators were the heroes of the time and were said to have whetted

Left: The Amphitheatre at Pompeii

114

Above: Helmets of gladiators unearthed near the amphitheatre

the sexual desires of many of the local women. Christians, as we know from the writings of later early Christian leaders such as Tertullian of Carthage and Clement of Alexandria, kept away from blood sports from the very beginning. They had respect for the life of both men, women and animals knowing that all were precious in the sight of God.

Bars and restaurants were numerous, and Pompeii has been estimated to contain about 150 bars and taverns selling either drink or hot foods. It is recognized that numbers of these bars would certainly have been involved in sex, prostitution and crimes of various kinds. The images on

the wall of the Bar of Salvius suggest an atmosphere of sex and drink. Another frequent activity in the bars would have been gambling. Although no gambling boards have yet come to light, there is evidence from the graffiti on the walls in some of the taverns that punters occasionally made quite large sums of money.

Shops and small businesses offered a whole range of produce including wine, fish sauce, lamps, perfumes and jewellery. There were also businesses engaged in building, metalwork and shoemaking and at least one bank has come to light in the excavations. In a city the size of Pompeii, whose population was in the region of 20,000, it comes as no surprise that more than thirty bakeries have been identified. Of particular interest is the bakery that was situated on the Via

Right:
House of the Chaste Lovers Bakery

dell'Abbondanza, one of the city's main thoroughfares. It is known as the **House of the Chaste Lovers** on account of frescoes on the wall depicting a feasting couple engaging in some rather coy kissing.

There is also a painting on one of the walls depicting a naked Venus admiring her reflection in a mirror. On the front façade of the shop there was a fresco of a bearded Mercury wearing a crown and with an extended phallus. This is now housed in the museum at Naples. Figurines and wall paintings emphasising the phallus are common in Pompeii, and presumably elsewhere in Roman cities, which illustrates the sex-driven culture among which the early Christians lived. This two-story business both milled the grain and baked the bread. The wheat or corn was poured into the tops of the mills which were made from volcanic stone. Slaves and donkeys were then used to turn the upper portion which ground the grain. Curved pans were placed on the ledges to collect the flour.

In addition to the bars which offered sex on the side **brothels** perhaps numbered as many as thirty or so. Archaeologist point out that it is not always easy to identify a brothel with certainty. So the picture of a couple making love on a bed chamber close to the kitchen, may simply have been an added source of income to the owners who were craftspeople

or retail traders. Sex was a significant recreational activity in Roman society and sexual partners could be of either sex. With a few exceptions, women were very much second class citizens and not in control of their own lives. Marital faithfulness was not seen as a virtue in Roman society and influential men regarded sex as their right to power and pleasure. The bodies of slaves and those at the lowest level of the social hierarchy were regarded by the rich as theirs by right.

The Lupanare was the main brothel of Pompeii and is situated close to the Stabian Baths. It had ten small chambers replete with stone beds, five of which were situated on the ground floor and five larger ones on the first floor which could be reached from a separate back entrance. Phalluses engraved on the road surfaces and on the facades of some of the houses directed people to the premises. In the entrance area there are a series of erotic

Above: A fast food outlet where fish sauce was sold

wall paintings which graphically depict men and women making love in various positions which was possibly a way of showing customers what was on offer. Many of them scratched their opinion of the performance of the prostitutes on the walls of the building. Against this background, common to all Roman cities, it is not surprising that Paul reminded the young Christians that their bodies belonged to the Lord and that they must never be united to a prostitute (1 Corinthians 6:13–20), and warned against sexual immorality (1 Thessalonians 4:3–8).

Above: Lupanare brothel

The Baths were intended for relaxation, recreation and social meetings. Almost everybody, including some slaves, went to the baths. They were also often places where morality was relaxed as bathers went into the water partially or totally unclothed. The baths were therefore often reputed to be places of sexual activity. This fact is well illustrated by scenes depicting sexual intercourse on the upper section of one of the walls in the changing room. Just over a century later Clement, a Christian leader from Alexandria, warned his fellow believers, that 'the baths are opened promiscuously to men and women; and there they

Left: Picture of the Via dell' Abbondanza from the Porta Marina. Notice the raised pavements

Right: Tepidarium
Stabian Baths

Below: The calidarium at
the Forum Baths

strip for licentious
indulgence, as if their
modesty had been
wasted in the bath.'

In early times Pompeii received
its water supply from the River
Sarno and from springs, but as
the city's population grew, an
aqueduct was constructed to
carry the water to the public
baths as well as to the homes of
some of the wealthier citizens.
Excavations have revealed the
large lead pipes that ran under the
pavements.

In Pompeii there are three main
baths: the Stabian, the Forum and
Central Baths. Here the public
could engage in such activities
as gymnastics, swimming and
sweating in a steam room.

The Stabian Baths included,
among other things, an exercise
area, a hot room, a plunge pool
and a swimming pool. The heat
was generated by a wood-burning
area which passed the heat under
the floors to the areas where it
was needed.

The Forum Baths are so
named on account of their
proximity to the Forum. They
are located at the junction of
Via del Foro and Via di Nola
and were built soon after the
Roman conquest about 80 BC.
These baths had a communal
central heating plant but separate

areas for men and women. The
facilities included hot, warm,
cold (frigidarium) and steam
(calidarium) baths, a gymnasium
and an open air courtyard.

Temples

Temples were everywhere.
Christians citizens or visitors to
Pompeii would undoubtedly have
shared Paul's feelings who, when
he first visited Athens 'was greatly
distressed to see that the city was
full of idols' (Acts 17:16). Pompeii
was literally filled with temples of
gods and goddesses. Many of the
temples had a high platform area

called *cella* or *naos* which was the most sacred part of the building where the statues of the deities were placed.

Prominent among the temples were those of Aesculapius, Apollo, Fortuna, Isis, Jupiter, Mars, Minerva and Hercules, Saturn, Venus and Vesta. One researcher commented that the city contained literally thousands of images of these gods and goddesses. They are in every shape and size: some in bronze and others in stone, marble or ivory. Many were small representations crafted as household gods. The Christian idea that there was only one God rather than many would have been anathema to first century Roman citizens; Christians were dubbed 'atheists' on account of their refusal to acknowledge the Roman deities and were accused of following a 'foreign superstition'.

The Roman state believed that their pantheon of gods protected both the state and the empire and they therefore paid particular respect to the major deities and their festivals. Many of the temple priests had no pastoral responsibilities and followed secular employment. They did not perform marriage ceremonies since the Roman practice was that living together for a year constituted marriage. This in itself must also have been a major challenge to Christians who sealed their marriages before Christ in a lifelong pledge of faithfulness (Romans 7:2)—clearly in sharp contrast to those of their neighbours.

The small **Temple of Isis** was first unearthed during an excavation in 1764. Located immediately next to the Theatre, the Temple was dedicated to the Egyptian goddess, Isis, and

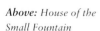

Above: *House of the Small Fountain*

Right: *The Temple of Isis*

for this reason sacred water from the Nile was kept in an underground passage below the building. Unsurprisingly the principal worshippers would have been women who worshipped a compassionate deity who offered salvation and life beyond the grave.

The building was clearly designed so that the members could get together for communal activities. There was a kitchen and dining area. The altar is outside in the courtyard. This temple, which was rebuilt after the earthquake of AD 62 with funds from Popidius Celsinus, is the best preserved temple in the city. There is a room behind the temple which was a meeting place for the initiates. Paintings and sculptures found in the excavations are now located in the Archaeological Museum in Naples. Mozart visited the temple of Isis in 1769 a few years after it was first excavated, and his memories of the site are said to have inspired him in his composition of the Magic Flute.

The Temple of Jupiter was built in the second century BC in honour of Jupiter, the ruler of the gods, and therefore it was the main centre of the religious life of the city. It was damaged in the earthquake of AD 62 after which it was rebuilt on a smaller scale. A large head of Jupiter was unearthed in the temple but is now housed in the Archaeological Museum in Naples.

The Temple of Apollo is an integral part of the Forum and was built in the third century BC; it is rectangular in design and bordered by 48 columns. There is a central altar, also surrounded by columns, and two statues one of Apollo shooting his arrows and one of his twin sister Diana the Huntress.

Top: *Temple of Jupiter with Vesuvius in the distance*

Above: *Temple of Apollo with statue of Apollo*

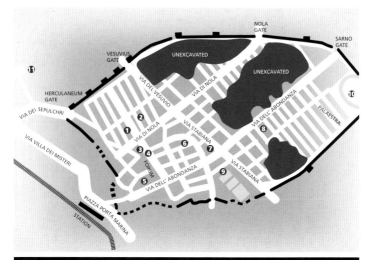

PLAN OF POMPEII LOCATING EACH OF THE RECOMMENDED PLACES

1 THE HOUSE OF THE TRAGIC
2 THE HOUSE OF THE FAUN
3 THE FORUM BATHS
4 THE TEMPLE OF JUPITER
5 THE TEMPLE OF APOLLO

6 THE LUPANARE BROTHEL
7 THE STABAIN BATHS
8 THE HOUSE OF THE
   CHASTE LOVERS

9 THE TEMPLE OF ISIS
10 THE AMPHITHEATRE
11 THE VILLA OF THE
   MYSTERIES

TRAVEL INFORMATION

Pompeii is easily reached by train from Rome changing at Naples and alighting at the Stazione Porta Marina. It takes approximately two hours and forty minutes on a standard class train and costs about twenty euros return if you book the day before and take a designated train. The journey can be completed in a shorter time on a first class train but the cost is four times as much.

The opening hours are from 8.30 am to 5.00 pm 1 November to 31 March, and 8.30 am to 7.30 pm 1 April–31 October. Tickets are free for European citizens who are under 18 or over 65 years of age. On arrival a walk along the Via dell' Abbondanza will help to give an immediate taste of the atmosphere of the place. There is a large self-service restaurant close to the Forum where the only toilets in the main area can be found. Pompeii can be very hot particularly in the summer months and so it is important to take a bottle of water which can be refilled from one of the many water taps. Restaurants can be expensive so it may be wise to bring a packed lunch. It is wise to wear good flat shoes and to hire an audio guide.

For further information contact info@ pompeiisites.org or infopompei@tin.it

Above: *The Forum Pompeii*

Left: Detail from the Forum Pompeii

Archaeological Museum in Naples

The Naples National Museum contains a large collection of Roman artefacts from Pompeii. These include bronzes in mint condition, mosaics, statues and wall paintings. There are a number of busts of Roman emperors and a large collection of Egyptian artefacts assembled by Cardinal Borgia in the late eighteenth century. If you are staying in the area a visit to the Museum would be very worthwhile. However, it is best to visit Pompeii first in order to get a feel for what is in the museum. Address: Piazza Museo 19, 80135 Naples, Italy or by ☎ 0039 081 440166, fax 0039 081 440013 or Email: archeon@arti. beniculturali.it

Above: Roman Road in Pompeii. Notice the pavements and traffic calming!

Left: A necropolis in Pompeii outside Porta Nocera

Right: The second century BC Ponte Rotto bridge

Roman history timeline 800 BC to AD 500

735–715	Romulus
616–597	Tarquinius Priscus
565	Servian Wall around Rome
510	Temple of Jupiter
312	Appian Way constructed
246–241	Punic Wars
234–83	Publius Scipio overcame the Carthaginians and defeated Hannibal
146	Romans conquer Greece
100–44	Julius Caesar
62	Ponte Fabricio constructed
51	Caesar conquers Gaul
27–14	Augustus
14–37	Tiberius
37–41	Caligula
41–54	Claudius
54–68	Nero
64	Fire destroys much of Rome
69–79	Vespasian
72	Colosseum
79	Eruption of Mount Vesuvius
79–81	Titus
81–96	Domitian
96–98	Nerva
98–117	Trajan
130	Hadrian's Wall completed
160–180	Marcus Aurelius
180–192	Commodus
222–235	Alexander Severus
270–275	Aurelian
270	Aurelian Walls begun
284–305	Diocletian
284	Empire divided East and West
312	Battle of Milvian Bridge
313	Edict of Milan
361–363	Julian the Apostate
378–395	Theodosius
407	Roman troops leave Britain
455	Rome sacked by Vandals
475	Fall of the Roman Empire
475–476	Romulus Augustus
500	Romulus defeated by the German chieftain, Odacer, and Western Roman empire comes to an end

Above: Victor Emmanuel

Timeline of key Christian events

c 42	Peter in Rome
65	Persecution under Nero
68	Martyrdom of Peter and Paul
70	Fall of Jerusalem
c 100	Martyrdom of Clement
c 117	Martyrdom of Ignatius
165	Martyrdom of Justin
235	Martyrdom of Hippolytus
c 250	Novatian consecrated as a rival bishop of Rome
312	Battle of Milvian Bridge
313	Edict of Toleration
320	Building of St Peter's
325	Council of Nicaea
381	Theodosius makes Christianity the official religion of the Roman Empire
435	Gladiatorial games ended
451	Council of Chalcedon
480–550	St Benedict
496	Pope Anastasius takes the title 'Pontifex Maximus'
609	Pantheon consecrated as a church
800	Charlemagne crowned Holy Roman Emperor by Pope Leo III in St Peter's
961	Otto becomes Holy Roman Emperor and Italy becomes part of the Holy Roman Empire
1108	San Clemente is rebuilt
1300	First Holy Year proclaimed by Pope Clement V
1378–1417	Great Papal Schism
1417	Council of Constance end Papal Schism
1473	Sistine Chapel completed
1475	Birth of Michelangelo
1483	Birth of Raphael
1510	Martin Luther's visit to Rome
1527	Emperor Charles V sacks Rome
1571	Birth of Caravaggio
1Z26	St Peter's Basilica completed
1633	Galileo condemned as a heretic
1735	Spanish Steps designed
1763	Trevi Fountain completed
1850	Pope Pius IX (1846–1878)
1854	Doctrine of the Immaculate Conception of the Virgin Mary
1861	Garibaldi takes Naples
1861	Victor Emmanuel II becomes King of Italy
1869–70	Vatican I Papal Infallibility decreed
1891	Leo XIII's Rerum Novarum Encyclical
1911	Victor Emmanuel Monument completed
1915	Italy enters World War I
1922	Mussolini becomes Premier
1929	Vatican State created
1944	Allies liberate Italy
1946	King Umberto II exiled. Italy becomes a Republic
1950	Doctrine of the Assumption of Mary decreed
1962–65	Vatican II
1975	Treaty of Rome inaugurates Common Market
2004	New EU constitution signed in Rome
2005	Pope John Paul II dies in Rome

Above: The Trevi Fountain is Rome's grandest and most famous fountain. There is a superstition that visitors who thrown a coin in the fountain are ensured a return

Roman Emperors

	Page	
Julius	45–44 BC	23, 95
Augustus	AD 27–14	23, 47, 95
Tiberius	14–37	31
Claudius	41–54	
Gaius (Caligula)	37–41	57, 59
Nero	54–68	24, 87
Vespasian	66–69	37
Titus	79–81	97
Domitian	81–96	24, 29, 104
Nerva	96–98	95
Trajan	98–117	95, 101
Hadrian	118–125	48, 64
Septimus Severus	193–211	96, 103
Diocletian	284–305	15, 99
Theodosius I	347–395	34, 89, 93
Constantine	306–337	5, 16-19, 26
Valentinian II	371–392	90
Arcadius	395–408	90
Romulus Augustulus	475–476	24

Select list of Bishops of Rome

		Page
Peter		8, 58
Linus	(67–76)	13
Anacletus	(76–88)	13
Clement	(88–97)	9, 10, 75
Callistus	(217–222)	86
Fabian	(236–250)	
Melchiades	(311–314)	
Silvester	(314–335)	69, 90
Innocent I	(402–417)	21
Leo I	(440–461)	21, 25
Gregory I	(590–604)	
Gregory II	(715–731)	
Leo III	(c750–815)	25
Leo IV	(847–855)	
Innocent III	(1198–1216)	
Nicholas III	(1277–1281)	
Urban VI (Rome)	(1378–1379)	
Clement VII (Avignon)	(1378–1394)	
Boniface IX (Rome)	(1389–1404	
Benedict XIII (Avignon	(1394–1422)	
Innocent VII (Rome)	(1404–1406)	
Gregory XII	(1406–1415)	
Alexander V	(1409–1414)	
Martin V (Rome)	(1417–1431)	70
Sixtus IV	(1471–1484)	55
Julius II	(1503–1513)	
Leo X	(1513–1521)	
Clement VII	(1523–1534)	
Paul IV	(1555–1559)	45, 46
Paul V	(1605–1621)	105
Pius IX	(1846–1878)	
Leo XII	(1873–1903)	
Pius XI	(1922–1939)	27, 62
Leo XIII	(1873–1903)	70
Pope John Paul II	(1978–2005)	
Pope Benedict XVI	(2005–)	

Select list of Christian leaders mentioned in this book

Painters and sculptors in Rome

Above: *Ice cream on Tiber Island!*

For the traveller to Rome

In order to visit all the sites in this guide you will need six clear days. If you are travelling from the United Kingdom it is probably best to leave about midday and arrive in Rome for the early evening. This will enable you to start out first thing the following morning. There are frequent flights from UK airports to Rome Ciampino. Some budget airlines provide a return coach journey from the airport to the centre of the city for a modest cost. There are also flights from Heathrow direct to Fiumicino (Leonardo da Vinci) airport from where there are frequent train services to Termini in the city centre.

Rome is best visited in the months of March to May and September to October. At other times it can be very hot reaching the high eighties Fahrenheit. The city has a large number of Pension hotels and there are also a number of small Christian hostels run by the Roman Catholic Church. They are clean and basic with most offering en suite facilities. It is not advisable to take travellers' cheques as few banks are willing to change them. It is not sensible to carry large sums of money since Rome is plagued by pickpockets. The best way is simply to use a cashpoint card in the local banks and carry as little cash as possible.

Index of place names

ACKNOWLEDGEMENTS

The author is grateful to Rob Binks, Ben Booth, Sheila Bowden, Giles Carpenter, Arthur Champion, Andrew and Rachel Hawkins, Bruce and Rosemary Clifford, Keith Holland and Agnes Walkowicz who provided photographs.

The following permissions are gratefully acknowledged: Capitoline Museum for Eros, Jupiter and Nero; Vatican Museum for The Battle of Milvian Bridge; Villa Borghese for Bernini's David and Scipione Borghese; John Paul Getty Museum for Canaletto's Colosseum; Real Academia de la Historia for Missorium Theodosius and Carlsberg Glyptotek, Copenhagen for Caligula.

Every effort has been made to identify copyright holders for the pictures in this book. Sincere apologies are offered for any unintentional omissions which will be inserted in any new editions.

RECOMMENDED READING

Akins, L., and Adkins, R.A, *Handbook to Life in Ancient Rome* (Oxford: OUP, 1994)

Beard, M., *Pompeii The Life of a Roman Town* (London: Profile Books, 2009)

Fagiolo, M., *Bernini* (Firenze: Scala, 1981)

Lanciani, R., *Pagan and Christian Rome* (Cambridge: Riverside Press, 1893)

Mancinelli, F., *The Catacombs of Rome and the Origins of Christianity* (Firenze: Scala, 1981)

O'Grady, D., *The Victory of the Cross* (London: HarperCollinsReligious, 1991)

Ushher, K., *Heroes, Gods and Emperors from Roman Mythology* (New York: Peter Bedrick Books, 1992)

Vicchi, A., *The Major Basilicas of Rome* (Firenze: Scala, 1999)

Wilken, R., *The Christians as the Romans Saw Them* (New Haven: Yale University Press, 1986)

AUTHOR

Nigel Scotland has spent the greater part of his life lecturing in church history at what became the University of Gloucestershire. He has been involved in church planting and since 2006 has taught theology students of Bristol Baptist College and Trinity College Bristol. Nigel is the author of more than a dozen books mostly on Christian history. His wife Liz died in 2010 and he has two married daughters and six grand children. He studied at McGill and Bristol Universities and earned a doctorate in Church History at the University of Aberdeen. His published work includes a study of the Lord's Supper in Early Christianity.